This book was personally chosen for

_____

Wishing you joy,

_____

Stride
Like a Lion

Soar
Like an Eagle

A Companion Guide
to *Living Joyously*

Elaine C. Scribner, BSN, RN, MPH, HSMI

Illustrated by Jim Armstrong

2 MOON Press

MARSHALL - MICHIGAN
800PUBLISHING.COM

Stride Like a Lion, Soar Like an Eagle

Copyright © 2012 by Elaine Scribner

Cover design by Kiernan Manion

Layout by Kait Lamphere

Author photo courtesy of author

The opinions expressed in this manuscript are solely the opinions of the author and do not represent the opinions or thoughts of the publisher. The author represents and warrants that s/he either owns or has the legal right to publish all material in this book.

ISBN-13: 978-1-938110-72-6

First published in 2012

10 9 8 7 6 5 4 3 2 1

Published by   2 MOON PRESS
123 W. Michigan Ave, Marshall, Michigan 49068
www.800publishing.com

All Rights Reserved. This book may not be reproduced, transmitted, or stored in whole or in part by any means, including graphic, electronic, or mechanical without the express written consent of the publisher except in the case of brief quotations embodied in critical articles and reviews.

PRINTED IN THE UNITED STATES OF AMERICA

For my daughter and her husband
With all my love

(¸.•´¸.•´¨) ¸.•*¨)
«´¨*... ☺ ...*¨`»
(¸.•´(¸.•´¨`•.¸)¨`•.¸)

Acknowledgements

I am grateful to the many people who have made this book possible. My sincerest thanks to my readers Keith Laidler, Richard Lassin, Jim Mandeville, and Rosalyn Routson, who gave generously of their time, insights, encouragement, and critiques. And Judy Scribner for her technical assistance with the document.

I am also deeply grateful to my many sources of inspiration, including The Dalai Lama, Lao Tzu, Thich Nhat Hanh, the Bible, Brian Luke Seaward, Henry Grayson, Paul Tillich, Harriet Goldhor Lerner, and many, many others.

My thanks to Jim Armstrong for his charming illustrations and his delight in life.

I am grateful to my parents who did the best they knew how, given many uncontrollable factors. A special thank you to the spirits of Alice Griswold and Floyd Young who encouraged and believed in me, sharing with me the precious gift of their time. And to the gentle spirit of Mark Holton.

My deepest gratitude to Joel Mpabwanimana and the many people who have enriched this book by letting me tell of their stories, their laughter and their words of wisdom.

And thank you to my wonderful daughter and her husband for being the inspiration, the blood, the sweat and the tears for this book. My special thanks to all of the people...my friends, co-workers, and students, who have challenged me to become a better person and have played with me as we learned together. And to the village of friends, church and family who supported me through the years and had a part in that lovely creation...my daughter.

Foreword

Perhaps more than any other time in the history of humanity, our twenty-first century lifestyles are filled with an abundance of stressful episodes, more commonly known as personal crises. Sages and spiritual luminaries remind us repeatedly that there are two ways you can deal with a personal crisis of stress; either as a victim or a victor. The stories of victims are quite common… and boring. Momentary grieving, over time, becomes a perpetual (and annoying) whine. Caught in a whirlpool of negativity, the victim lives the expression, "Once a victim, twice a volunteer."

Conversely, the stories of victors are inspiring, for they not only illuminate the remarkable triumph of the human spirit, but their fortunes of grace and dignity shed light on our paths as well, making our journey a bit easier. Renowned mythologist, Joseph Campbell described these stressful moments as "initiations" on the hero's journey. Each stressor offers a profound learning experience. Moreover, each episode of personal crisis offers us to move from a motivation of fear toward a motivation of love. This is the only way for the evolution of the soul growth process to occur. For many this shift appears a chasm too wide to cross; fear keeps them immobilized. Yet this move, this quantum leap, can be made with the mere turn of a thought, a shift in perception. There are many colors in love's rainbow. The book you hold in your hand is a metaphorical bridge over this abyss. This book is a gift. In accepting this gift you will find in your hands nothing less than a pot of immeasurable gold.

Elaine Scribner is no stranger to stress on her Hero's Journey. Her path of trials proved to be extremely challenging, yet her determination to make the journey "home" as a victor is nothing less than heroic, transformational and inspiring. Campbell reminds us that it is incumbent on the Hero's Journey, when one returns home, to share what they have learned with their community. In doing so, the hero becomes what Joseph Campbell calls the "master of two worlds," the world they conquered, and the world they return home to. Upon the return home we celebrate the victory of success. Success on the hero's journey is yet another color in love's rainbow. Some say success is the entire rainbow itself.

Elaine is one such master, and like the gift of a map and compass, she shares her collective wisdom with you in these pages so that you too may choose the path of the victor on your own hero's journey. Given the state of the world today, we don't need any more victims. We need heroes, people who can rise to the challenges that face them and reach their highest potential each and every day.

You will find that the hero's journey is a profound metaphor for the human journey, also called the spiritual path. The spiritual path is not one measured in years, miles or possessions, (though many sure try the later). Perhaps the spiritual path is best measured in experiences though this seems unlikely too. There are some who say that the spiritual path is nothing more than 12-14 inches long. Really you say? Yes! It is the distance from your head to your heart. It is this very distance that Elaine guides you through with a series of wonderful exercises that will take you to the top of the proverbial mountain to get a clear view of where your journey will next take you so you too can make it back home safely. You are in the hands of a wonderful guide, who truly understands the healing and transformational power of love. Live well and love deeply. It truly is the only way back home.

Brian Luke Seaward, Ph.D.
The Paramount Wellness Institute
Boulder, Colorado

Contents

INTRODUCTION 1

Section I. THE ART OF LIVING WELL

1. LIVING WELL 11
2. SPIRITUALITY AND LOVE 21

Section II. 21ST CENTURY TOOLS

3. THE POWER OF WORDS 35
4. THE POWER OF SPIRITUALITY 53
5. THE POWER OF LOVE 69
   - COMPASSION 70
   - KINDNESS 73
   - FORGIVENESS 75
6. BALANCE 87
   - "THE ENOUGHNESS PRINCIPLE" 88
   - SIMPLICITY 88
   - SLEEP 91
   - TIME MANAGEMENT 95
   - WORK 96
   - MONEY MATTERS 96
   - EXERCISE 97
   - NUTRITION…Changing Habits 101
   - LAUGHTER and PLAY 104
   - VOLUNTEERING 111
   - STRONG EMOTIONAL REACTIONS 111

Section III. RELATIONSHIPS

7. RELATIONSHIP WITH SELF 121
8. RELATIONSHIP WITH THE DIVINE 125

9. FAMILY RELATIONSHIPS 127
10. RELATIONSHIPS AT WORK 135
11. HOW TO STAY IN LOVE (PRACTICALLY) FOREVER 141

Section IV. SPEED BUMPS

12. HOW STRESS WORKS 159
13. A WORD ABOUT FEAR 165
14. EXPECTATIONS 179
    Barriers 182
    Change 185
    Strong Emotional Reactions 187
    Worry and Fear 189
    Perspectives on Unemployment,
       Underemployment or Job Dissatisfaction 190
    Maturational Changes 191
    Illness and Pain 192
    A Word About Grief 194

Section V. ARE WE THERE YET?

15. TAKING ACTION 201
16. THE FRUITS OF LIVING WELL:
    STORIES AND WORDS OF WISDOM 205

Section VI. APPENDICES and FUN STUFF

Appendix I   Choosing a Therapist........................ 219
Appendix II   Maslow's Hierarchy (Elaine's Version).......... 221
Appendix III   Abusive Realtionships 223
Afterword and Momisms
References and Resources
Index

Exercises

SECTION I. THE ART OF LIVING WELL

1. LIVING WELL 11
   - Exercise 1.1 Living Well Questionnaire 12
   - Exercise 1.2 Be a Swan 13
   - Exercise 1.3 Gremlins and Boggarts 14
   - Exercise 1.4 My Living Joyously Plan 20
2. SPIRITUALITY AND LOVE 21
   - Exercies 2.1 What Animates Your Life? 23
   - Exercise 2.2 Guiding Principles 24

SECTION II. 21ST CENTURY TOOLS

   - Exercise 3.1 The Yah-But Exercise 33
3. THE POWER OF WORDS 35
   - Exercise 3.2 An Attitude of Gratitude 39
   - Exercise 3.3 Refocus Tools For Stinkin'-thinkin'/
     Mud-mind Times 40
   - Exercise 3.4 Magical Moments -- The Happy Thoughts Card .. 41
   - Exercise 3.5 How to Create Affirmations 42
   - Exercise 3.6 So Write Already! Journaling tips...
     pick which ones work for you 46
   - Exercise 3.7 Conscious Listening 50
   - Exercise 3.8 The Daily Family Powwow 51
4. THE POWER OF SPIRITUALITY 53
   - Exercise 4.1 Creating a Sanctuary 55
   - Exercise 4.2 Smile Meditation 60
   - Exercise 4.3 The Eagle Meditation 60
   - Exercise 4.4 Being in the Moment 65
   - Exercise 4.5 Conscious Hugging 66
   - Exercise 4.6 Continuous Mindfulness 66

5. THE POWER OF LOVE 69
    Exercise 5.1   *Enrich Your Life:*
                           Practice Random Acts of Kindness 74
    Exercise 5.2   *Emotional Tranquility Meditation Exercise* 76
    Exercise 5.3   *Nine Steps Toward Forgiveness* 79
    Exercise 5.4   *Give It Some Thought* 81

6. BALANCE 87
    Exercise 6.1   *Time Management Grid* 96
    Exercise 6.2   *Centered Silliness* 107
    Exercise 6.3   *Stormy Weather – Journaling* 112
    Exercise 6.4   *Yah-But Revisited* 113

SECTION III. RELATIONSHIPS

7. RELATIONSHIP WITH SELF: Being Happy and Whole 121
8. OUR RELATIONSHIP WITH THE DIVINE 125
9. FAMILY RELATIONSHIPS 127
    Exercise 9.1   *The Powwow: Family Meeting Guidelines* 131
10. RELATIONSHIPS AT WORK 135
    Exercise 10.1   *Be a Swan at Work* 139
11. HOW TO STAY IN LOVE [PRACTICALLY] FOREVER 141
    Exercise 11.1   *Conscious Listening Revisited* 149
    Exercise 11.2   *Mindful Breathing* 150

SECTION IV. SPEED BUMPS

12. HOW STRESS WORKS 159
13. A WORD ABOUT FEAR 165
    Exercise 13.1   *Creating a Sanctuary Revisited* 169
    Exercies 13.2   *Count Your Blessings* 175
    Exercise 13.3   *Choose Your Attitude – Journal Topic* 177
    Exercise 13.4   *Choose Your Action – Journal Topic –*
                            Choose to Act, Not React 177

14. EXPECTATIONS ... 179
Exercise 14.1 Expectations Journal ... 180
Exercise 14.2 Its Time Will Come ... 182
Exercise 14.3 Values, Barriers and Strengths Journal Topic .. 184
*Exercise 14.4 Journal Topic: What Areas do I Need to
                Concentrate on to Get Where I Want to Go?* ... 185
Exercise 14.5 Tie One On ... 188

INTRODUCTION

> "Life is a test. It is only a test. If this had been your actual life, you would have been given better instructions."
>
> *Bumper Sticker*

We are more than our jobs, our fears, our debt. Life woke me up to this in my early 30s, when, within five years, LIFE happened in capital letters. When my daughter was 3 years old, I was diagnosed with melanoma. With a life expectancy of five years, my priorities in life began to change. Two years later, my mother was diagnosed with stage-four lung cancer. I was living 1,200 miles away from my family at the time, with just a three-year lease on life myself. I returned home to care for her and be with my family. My husband chose to remain in Houston. My mother died six months later. My marriage dissolved, and just as I was reestablishing myself with a job and a home, I was laid off twice within two years.

I affectionately call this time frame the beginning of my Journey to Joy. It is now 23 years this November since this tumultuous journey began, and I am still joyful. I have learned that when chaos hits, I can reestablish joy, peace and contentment. It was not a pain-free process, and though I value every lesson learned, I wish I might have had a book such as this that would pose a whole gamut of strategies to pick and choose from. I might have chosen differently. I say this, even though I am content with where I am now.

Life is definitely challenging, often rampant with unpredictability and sometimes frightening precariousness, but we *can* live joyously -- despite the pain, grief, stressors both mental and emotional, threats to health and safety, and the assorted speed bumps that life sends our way. One of my favorite quotes is from a novel in which the main character tells a very unhappy young woman, that "there is no happily ever after…there are only happy people" (Gilman). The only thing in this world that we can change is our own attitude. So, being joyous and happy is a choice for which we must take personal action. Every morning we create our reality. We can choose the path that leads to happiness. Certainly there will be days when it is hard -- days when the big stuff happens and grief and depression seem inevitable. But even while wallowing in darkness, I still had the assurance that happiness *will* prevail, that time *will* heal. I just needed to do everything I knew until time did its work. I had the choice to be victim or victor. Even when I sought help, it was a positive affirmation that happiness and joy were mine for the asking, an acknowledgement that this is just a speed bump.

I began writing this book when my daughter was one year from graduating from college and became engaged. I had 2 ½ years before the wedding to prepare this send-off. There was still time to feed her brain and her heart, and teach her the skills of living well and being happy. It is a mother's hope, a mother's legacy: be happy, live joyously. Not just joyfully but effervescently, contagiously joyous.

Wherever you are on your life journey, I wish you welcome and thank you for letting me be a part of it. New beginnings are often fraught with uncertainty and fear, despite all their initial promise. Maybe it is a new job, a new phase in a relationship such as getting married or embarking on parenthood, settling into a new home or neighborhood, taking on eldercare or starting retirement. Perhaps life has just come to a standstill and you are seeking something else, not sure what that is but feeling unsettled and disquieted. Perhaps you are simply coping with life, grieving, depressed, seemingly rocked by every wave in the ocean of experience and tired of being merely functional. Maybe life seems like a perpetual emotional rollercoaster, a never ending drama. Or, too often for comfort, that sinking feeling comes, that little voice that whispers in your ear, "How long can this last?" "When will the other shoe drop?" "This is too good to be true."

It may simply be that you need to look inward and learn to listen to your own wisdom to find your path to happiness. Or you may feel that a total derailing and starting anew is called for, but you don't want to admit defeat. You will learn that this is the voice of the ego. You will learn how to quiet it so you can hear your own wisdom, find your own path and harness it to achieve your goals. You will learn how to find peace, happiness and contentment, with or without the derailment you may have envisioned. When LIFE happens, there *IS* a way to find balance and to be whole, happy and clear thinking throughout. You will find balance and learn to be resilient. We all have moments of despair, grief, anger, anxiety and uncertainty, but it is how quickly we regain our balance that determines our happiness and well-being.

Even happy events can be stressful. The birth of a baby, no matter how welcome or joyous the event, is stressful. Sympathy abounds for new parents when they first feel that instant of gut-wrenching fear: "OMG, there's no going back." After all, not only do babies not come with a manufacturer's instruction book -- they are non-returnable! When my only child was about 1 to 2 weeks old, I was distraught when I called my mother. My daughter was all scrunched up in her baby seat as I wailed, "What you do with babies? She just sits there like a frog."

Not only that, but she was incontinent at both ends, and every now and then she would get this look of Captain Bligh, with the index finger of her right hand up, one eye closed, mouth open. It was probably gas. I was a little stressed. As predicted, we both made it, and not only that, we thrived.

There must be something better I can do to prepare her....

And I ask you, do we then turn around and send these same children out into life at 18 or 21 without an instruction book? Not in my book we don't! When my daughter, her friends and then my nephews went off to college, I gave them the book *"Take Care Of Yourself,"* a decision-tree-style book to help them take care of their physical health. Then, when my daughter became engaged, I knew that I could not do any less for her emotional, mental and spiritual health.

My thinking was that I may have given her a lot of wisdom to live happily, but will she remember it? My own mother gave me just three pieces of advice/wisdom that I can remember:

1. *"What's the worst that can happen?"* (when I was stressed about things she told me to ask myself this).
2. *"Life is tough, then you die."*
3. And when I become engaged to be married: *"Just make sure it's not lust."*

The first one has actually had a lot of value for me through the years, but the other two are grim Scots/English heritage at its best. "Just make sure it's not lust" may actually have a lot of meat to it, but at 23 years of age, I needed advice that was a little more concrete. I just didn't know what I didn't know. Unfortunately, I didn't really get to know my mother as an adult, because I moved 1,200 miles away out of college and she died when I was in my early 30s. There may have been more wisdom there, but time, space and circumstances prohibited developing the mother-daughter relationship that I now would cherish.

So the question remains, what will our children remember as they embark on life, be it across town or 2,200 miles away? And did we get the information right the first time? And even if we did, how did they internalize it? After all, they saw it through the eyes of a child and probably got only part of the story. If there is any doubt that children perceive things differently, listen to this next story which happened when I was about 5 years old. Through the eyes of a child things can be very magical indeed.

Through the Eyes of a Child

I was born in Arlington, Massachusetts, just outside of Boston. We lived on the second floor of a two-family home, and we had at least one hurricane that I vaguely remember. When I was 7, we moved to Michigan, and I had no further experience with hurricanes until I married and moved to Houston, Texas. And there we were, August 1983. I was in our second-story apartment preparing for hurricane Alicia. She was in the Gulf, heading straight for us, packing winds of 125 mph. I was puttering around, listening to the news and weather, gathering candles, flashlights and duct tape, while they were going over things to do to be prepared. I distinctly remember standing in front of the television, and then, as I started moving off into the hallway, I can still see that rust-colored carpeting and the white adobe-textured walls as they told us to fill our tubs with water. Then, flashback: I was 7 years old and watching my mother prepare for the hurricane that was heading our way. She was filling the tub with water, and I knew, I just knew, with that sense of awe that a child feels when she puts 2 and 2 together and gets 8. It was to hold the house down. It was infinitely and intuitively logical. I was pretty impressed with myself...at 7 years old, I had the world all figured out. Then, in a flash, I was back in 1983 and I immediately laughed. I was 27 years old and no, it was not to hold the house down -- it was for water to flush toilets and wash your hands.

We still have that same magical thinking when it comes to living well. It should be so easy, so natural, so intuitively logical. But the evidence shows us that the world is more complicated than this. The information age has put more knowledge at our fingertips in one day than people had in a lifetime 100 years ago. But the skills that once allowed us to live as a family have not kept pace. With life expectancy in 1800 only 25 years, marriages were short. The same skills do not seem to be keeping us together through mid-life crises, empty nest and into old age. And what about happiness for those who never marry or remarry? Are they doomed to be forever striving for happiness with that special someone, or is happiness and contentment within their reach as well?

Further, if living well and being happy were intuitively logical, why is depression occurring in pandemic proportions? Why are 40 to 50 percent of marriages ending in divorce? Is it hopeless? How can we guide our children when we have not modeled happiness very well ourselves? The information and skills we have about living well have generally been limited to or based on observations of our circle of family and friends. Most of our observations were while we were children and colored by magical thinking. All of which limits and even skews our view of the tools it takes to live well, to live joyously.

So, how can we be happy despite circumstances, despite those elements that seem to conspire toward a bad day? Can we remain empowered? Where can we find an inner peace that cannot be disturbed? How can we maintain a clear mind and a loving, joyful heart?

How to Use This Book

This is a guidebook for new beginnings. It synthesizes ageless wisdom about living well and living joyously, and the new physics of love. It is part self-exploration and part how-to. When I am struggling with something, sometimes it is enough for me just to hear someone else say the same thing I have been thinking. Sometimes clarification and redefinition are enough. For other issues, there are exercises for practice and deeper self-exploration as well as resources to direct you further. One of my readers said it is not a book that you just read -- it is a book that you do.

I would encourage you to read the first two chapters and the section on journaling first. Journaling can be a valuable tool on your journey *if* it fits your style. It may feel awkward at first, but give it a good try. After that, you may want to continue reading cover to cover or jump ahead to techniques you wish to learn first or issues of most concern to you. If you have no particular issues, just keep going.

The first section will give you the basics of living well, theories of love and ego, and a model for maintaining a clear mind and a loving heart. The second section will explore the skills and tools needed for joyous living. The third section deals with relationships: love of self, love of the divine and love of others. The last section is about the realities of applying these principles to real life and troubleshooting problem areas.

Most chapters have exercises so you can practice and incorporate the various techniques. As the list of tools and goals grows, you will certainly want to prioritize or even combine them. Plan to start with one easy task and one more challenging as a way to build your self-confidence. You may periodically want to pause in your reading until you have experienced some success with an identified area. Exercise 1.4 is your Living Joyously Plan, a model that you can use throughout the book to design your own journey to joy.

Changing is not easy. Practice is the key. Experts recommend that you spend five minutes most days with a skill to make it a habit. The closer it is to the same time and place in your daily schedule, the more likely you will remember it. I also use index cards as reminders, placing them in strategic locations to help my failing memory and reinforce my commitment to it. For example, I am currently striving to reestablish diet and exercise routines while still trying to establish a meditation routine for myself. I haven't yet found the right mix for this one (time, type, habit, etc). The plan is not to take on anything new until I have mastered these.

Prepare to push your comfort zone. Prepare to be silly. Prepare to sit still and meditate. These can be uncomfortable if you are not used to doing them. Growth occurs from stretching the boundaries of your comfort zone. Certainly you will find activities that simply do not suit you, but try them first. Just like Bill Murray in the movie "Groundhog Day," if you keep doing what you've always done, nothing will change -- you'll keep getting the same results. Maybe by changing ourselves, by brightening the corner where we are, by becoming more joyous, we can make a difference in the world. It is time for a new approach, for radical changes, even love. The Dalai Lama said in his book *How to see Yourself as you Really Are*, "basic human problems remain...we have not yet succeeded in bringing about peace and happiness or in reducing overall suffering." Peace begins at home, so we must start here because the only thing we can change is ourselves. Maybe then there will be hope for our world.

SECTION I

THE ART OF LIVING WELL

Chapter 1
LIVING WELL

> "If you realize that you have enough, you are truly rich."
> Tao Te Ching, v. 33 (translated by Wayne Dyer)

We are always seeking. Whether it is something new or more or different, it seems that by nature we human beings are questors. We are on a journey of discovery and often cannot let the dust settle or the grass grow and simply be content. When we look outside ourselves for satisfaction, we tend to turn this energy toward acquiring more. Like magpies, we want things that are better, brighter and more beautiful. Or we may become excitement or drama junkies, seeking outside ourselves for satisfaction. And when the novelty of these possessions or experiences wanes, we're likely ratchet up these behaviors. They become intensified until they are even more self-destructive...until we're numbing the pain of discontent with drugs, alcohol, food, gambling, shopping, sex, etc. The crux of the problem is that there is always more to be had that is better, brighter and more beautiful, and we may never be content. If we instead take our journey inward, toward self-discovery and love, there is infinite space, with no price tags, no expiration dates, no limits to be found. If you are willing to do the work, peace, joy and contentment *will* follow.

Survival no longer takes up most of our waking time. Daniel Pink, in his book *A Whole New Mind*, stipulates that with all our "material abundance [there is a] deepening of our nonmaterial yearnings." In other words, our quest for self-actualization and being the most we can be (A. Maslow).

The following exercise involves rating yourself on a continuum. I have provided some key questions and additional space for you to add your own. You can pull out some of the items listed to expand upon them if you need to, and as you read further, you can come back to this and add more -- whatever it takes, make this your tool.

EXERCISE 1.1 LIVING WELL QUESTIONNAIRE

Are you living well?

| Not at All | Could be better | OK | Enough | Excess |

[--]

Do you have enough food, housing, money?

| Not at All | Sometimes stressful | Enough | Excess |

[--]

Do you have enough leisure time, time with family and friends?

| Not at All | Could be better | Enough | Excess |

[--]

Are you happy?

| Not at All | Could be happier | Happy | Excess |

[--]

YOUR OWN: _____

| Not at All | Could be better | Enough | Excess |

[--]

YOUR OWN: _____

| Not at All | Could be better | Enough | Excess |

[--]

YOUR OWN: _____

| Not at All | Could be better | Enough | Excess |

[--]

There is no way to happiness…..
Happiness is the way

Thich Nhat Hanh

WHAT DO YOU HOPE FOR FROM LIFE?

What do you hope for regarding your family and relationships, your job or career? Take the time here to write it out. With activities such as this, I tend to use pencil, sticky-notes, write in the margins, use bullets. Do whatever works for you: type it, use additional paper, or even get a journal or notebook specifically for the exercises in this book.

EXERCISE 1.2   BE A SWAN

Describe a day of living well. What would it look like? How would it start and end? How would it look, smell, sound, feel and taste? Who would you choose to spend time with? Be as specific as you can be. Make it a 72-hour day if you need to! Consider money, family, play and hobbies, social, emotional and spiritual aspects. This is your perfect day. Dream it. Describe it. (P.S this is a day off work.)

_____

_____

_____

_____

_____

_____

[Note: EXERCISE 4.2 adapts this exercise for your workday.]

Put this in a prominent place (bedroom mirror, refrigerator) and review it daily. Don Coyhis, a Native American speaker and author, says, "You become that which you think about," so start thinking on it *NOW!* Watch as the pieces start creeping into your life.

EXERCISE 1.3 GREMLINS AND BOGGARTS

What keeps you from getting there?

STEP 1 - What are your gremlins, or in the Harry Potter books, your boggarts? Boggarts are those nasty little shape-shifters in your closet that take on your deepest fear. They are those little voices that say things like: "You can't write a book, there are too many on the shelves now," "People don't really read, let alone apply what they read," or "You can only write procedure manuals."

What are your gremlins or boggarts saying to you?

Boggart # 1: _____

Boggart # 2: _____

Boggart # 3: _____

STEP 2 - List a few ideas for dealing with these little voices when they rear their ugly heads. Music and songs are extremely helpful. Even if you sing it in your head, it fills all the empty or dark spaces with light and joy.

Ex: 1) Start singing/humming an uplifting song. (I like "Wind Beneath My Wings")

2) Pull out your Happy Thoughts card (See Ex. 2.4, Happy Thoughts Exercise).

_____

_____

_____

_____

Now, having defined what living well would look like for yourself and some of the things that are getting in your way, how can you make it happen? It seems as if it should be simple, but obviously with so much depression and divorce, we may have the head knowledge, but we certainly don't have the skills (or aren't using them) to sustain the effort.

To make change happen, you have to change the way you think. Sometimes a clear vision is all that is needed. And now that you have identified your gremlins and boggarts, it may be enough to say, "Put thee behind me" in whatever fashion works for you, and "just do it." These instances of clarity and resolve work magically when there is no dissonance between thought and action. You are able to make a decision that the past is gone and you are not going to let it ruin today. Sometimes it is simply enough to examine and acknowledge issues from your past long enough to gain insights into current behaviors. Example: "It was a bad time, I can see what I did to protect myself, but that behavior doesn't serve me anymore." Then make a decision *not to do that anymore*. And simply *be happy*. Then practice. With practice, the new habit of living well will get easier and easier, to the point where it is a natural and unconscious choice. To help your practicing, post your vision of living well somewhere where you can see it and recommit to it every day.

Sometimes you may need to do additional work with a counselor or therapist's help. Once you've exorcised those ghosts, be done with it. New theories and research are showing that telling and retelling the story is not only reliving it but living it today, with no room for the new, the bright, the beautiful, the here and now. Current research has found that catharsis, or releasing these pent-up emotions, does not relieve feelings but rather validates them and leads to greater emotional arousal. This is the basis of the relatively new Eye Movement Desensitization Reprogramming (EMDR), a therapy which releases the energy tied up in the trauma and allows the healing process to begin. If you do need therapy, write down your goals before hand, take your Be A Swan exercise (Ex. 1.2) with you, and choose a therapist knowledgeably (See Appendix 1 "Choosing a Therapist".)

Other times you may experience the feeling of being undeserving (this can be a hidden boggart) -- times when those little voices say,

"You can't" or "You should." Remember, you deserve to be happy and joyful. You are a child of God, a divine manifestation of creation. Our bodies are temples, holding the light of the divine. Care for your temple. It's simple, good sense, and also it's just plain good science. Research is finding that we are healthier when we are happy: heart, immune system and brain functioning are increased. We have more energy, we are stronger, more creative and more productive. A Hindu spiritual says, "While pain is inevitable, misery is optional." You have a right to be happy. Choose it. Practice it.

Several years ago, I had gone to a salon to get my hair cut, and while I was waiting I was idly thumbing through the magazines (the only time I ever get to do this). I found an article entitled "101 Ways to Put More Joy in Your Life." Its basic premise was that joy is a basic human need. Being the good nurse-educator that I am, I had been indoctrinated in nursing school on Maslow's hierarchy of human needs. I fussed and fumed over this terminology. Nowhere in Maslow's hierarchy is there joy (see Appendix 2). You can try to persuade yourself that a couple of the categories allude to it, but it truly is not there. In the classes and workshops I taught subsequently, I mentioned this article and this premise: it's not in there, but it *is* important.

Then I had an ah-ha moment. Joy *is* indeed a basic human need. It is perhaps the most important of them, as my friend Howard taught me.

> I met Howard when he was 84. He was volunteering for SCORE at the time, a group of retired executives who mentor business people. He was helping me write a business plan. I found out later that he had a doctorate, spoke and read four languages, was a meticulous woodworker, and had many other unique talents and abilities, but he was always quiet and self-deprecating about them.
>
> He enjoyed simple pleasures, such as cookies and milk with a friend. He loved charming but risqué jokes and would laugh self-consciously about them. Sitting

on his front porch, he would wave at the kids as they went off to school and as they came home. As the years went by, his activities became fewer (treasurer for this group, secretary for that one), but still, he enjoyed, as always, these simple pleasures.

One day Howard found that he had prostate cancer. He was taking the chemotherapy well but had become noticeably frailer. Still he was hanging onto his simple pleasures and waving at the kids every day and mowing his own lawn, albeit with frequent stops now. The cancer spread and he had to have surgery. He came home and was slowly regaining his strength when a couple of months later he spiked a fever. By the time he mentioned it to me, it seemed to have resolved itself.

Then, some time later, on the morning of the long-awaited wedding of a dear friend, he called me to tell me he again had a fever. He didn't want to miss this wedding, he said, and he wouldn't call the doctor until afterward. Not good. So I said to him, "OK, Howard, only for you will I put on a pair of nylons." So off we went to the wedding.

Predictably, the doctor ordered blood cultures and later that week he was hospitalized with MRSA, a life-threatening infection for the debilitated. A week later he called me from the hospital to tell me they wanted to put him in a nursing home to recover. That was Tuesday. Two days later he died.

There is no doubt in my mind that he lost his will to live. He saw the joy he took in the small things disappearing and lost hope. He had lost his joy in living.

Joy gives someone purpose and the will to live. Howard lost his joy and died shortly thereafter. When we have no food or water or shelter (Maslow's basic human needs), joy gives us the desire to seek these. If we have no joy, no hope, our spirit gives up. Joy, hope, love – these are the energies that power life itself.

Joy *is* a basic human need. Achieving joy requires a healthy, balanced, holistic approach. I grew up "knocking on wood" when good things happened or even when just speaking of good happenings. This is a Druid superstition that has entrenched itself in our society. Good things just happening is not the natural order of things. We must control the situation, we must make things happen. Both are illusions that we have control. We need a new vision, one that proclaims that we are indeed deserving of being happy, that seeking happiness is not selfish but divine. We need to find balance at work and play, in our social and spiritual lives, and in our love of self and others, and our need for a sense of purpose and leisure/play.

We need balance, simplicity, harmony, love, forgiveness and connectedness. Is it selfish on an airplane when it depressurizes to put your oxygen on first? No, you are better able to care for others. We need to exercise our "spiritual muscles," as Brian Luke Seaward calls them, and take care of ourselves. If we know our life to be out of balance, we need to use the tools at our disposal to bring it back into balance, and being joyous is perhaps the measure of our success. It is then that we and those around us will reap the fruits of living well to be happy and resilient.

The model below is a set of three mandalas that demonstrate the interrelatedness of the many facets of love and the resulting fruits that such balance can bring. All three are equally important. Neglect one and they all suffer. You are out of balance, as if limping through life with a flat tire (forgive the mixed metaphor).

A blank version of the model is provided for you to make your own plan. Determine what areas you need or want to work on. Identify activities that you need and want to do to ensure balance and joy. Use it as a reminder and guide. I would even suggest physically keeping it in front of you -- putting it on the bedroom mirror, write it on a notecard and put the card on the dashboard of your car or wherever you will see it often. Add to and subtract from it to make it a strong, viable and living plan.

Figure 1.1 Living Joyously Model
A Holistic Approach to Happiness and Living Well, Living Joyously

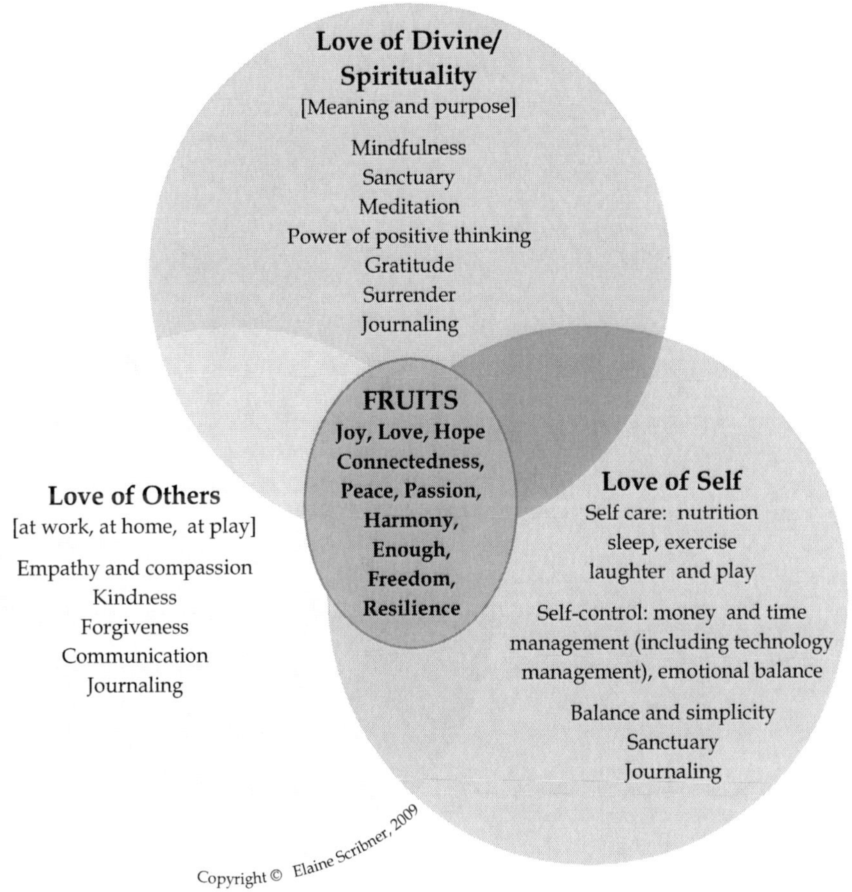

Love of Divine/ Spirituality
[Meaning and purpose]

Mindfulness
Sanctuary
Meditation
Power of positive thinking
Gratitude
Surrender
Journaling

FRUITS
Joy, Love, Hope
Connectedness,
Peace, Passion,
Harmony,
Enough,
Freedom,
Resilience

Love of Others
[at work, at home, at play]

Empathy and compassion
Kindness
Forgiveness
Communication
Journaling

Love of Self

Self care: nutrition
sleep, exercise
laughter and play

Self-control: money and time management (including technology management), emotional balance

Balance and simplicity
Sanctuary
Journaling

Copyright © Elaine Scribner, 2009

EXERCISE 1.4   MY LIVING JOYOUSLY PLAN

Love of Divine/ Spirituality
[Meaning and purpose]

_____

_____

_____

_____

Love of Others
[at work, at home, at play]

_____

_____

_____

_____

Love of Self
[Self care]

_____

_____

_____

_____

Copyright © Elaine Scribner, 2009

CHAPTER 2
SPIRITUALITY AND LOVE
Basic Precepts of a Joyous Life

......In Search of Meaning

> "The ideal life is not a fear-fueled pursuit of cheese. It's more like walking a labyrinth, where the purpose is the journey itself."
> *A Whole New Mind*, Daniel H. Pink

> "Resolve to put away your fears and find a more rewarding path."
> *The New Year's Quilt*, Jennifer Chiaverini

    We live in interesting times. We own more but have less. We have such abundance and yet are still thirsty, still hungry. And we seem to think that by acquiring more, we will fill that void. Victor Frankl, in his book *Man's Search for Meaning*, observes that "People have enough to live, but nothing to live for; they have the means but no meaning." He further observes "man's main concern is not to gain pleasure or to avoid pain but rather to see a meaning in his life." We have been looking outside of ourselves for an "easy fix." Barbara Kingsolver says it well in her article *"The Color Red"*: "Technology continues deluging us with information and industry with material things...choking us with choices. And yet, the realization *is* dawning...there *is* more. It's just not where we've been looking for it."

    We have been liberated by prosperity but not fulfilled by it.

Daniel Pink describes this era as that of postmaterialistic values, where "abundance has brought beautiful things, but this bevy of material goods has not necessarily made us much happier... [though it] has freed literally hundreds of millions from the struggle for survival."

Is spirituality going to church and Sunday school once a week? Or taking the kids to youth group? Is it carrying your Bible door to door to bring people to the light? Is it spending time with nature or shoveling your neighbor's driveway? These may be part of your personal practice of spirituality -- everyone's is different. Does that mean that the person who professes him/herself to be an atheist is not spiritual?

Being loving and compassionate *is* spirituality. Spirit, as defined by Merriam-Webster is "an animating or vital principle held to give life to physical organisms," and spirituality is "related to, or affecting the spirit." Therefore, being spiritual is giving attention to or being that which gives you life. So do the math. We know that God is love, so spirituality is giving attention to love.

In *A Whole New Mind,* Pink discusses that there is a growing awareness, fuelled by both the scientific and the spiritual communities, that a close relationship exists between the scientific and the spiritual. Eric Lander (2003 Scientist of the Year and director of MIT) and the Dalai Lama concurred that science is merely one way to understand the world. Further, Pope John Paul II said "science can purify religion from error and superstition. Religion can purify science from idolatry and false absolutes." One example of this is found in the fact that attending a place of worship positively affects longevity. Though that may be just a proxy measure for spirituality, it does demonstrate the value of spirituality in living well -- or at least living long.

EXERCISE 2.1   WHAT ANIMATES YOUR LIFE?

What animates your life? What is important to you? What gives you joy? What gives your life meaning and purpose?

List whatever comes to mind, even if it's not all-encompassing. Don't edit. It can be **general**: family, success, education, love your neighbor, do unto others, love. It can be **concrete**: a colorful piece of Native American weaving; an exhilarating hour in nature while cross-country skiing; seeing the light bulb go off in a student's eyes; being there when your grandchild calls from school to say, "Grampa, I think I left the curling iron plugged in, can you check it for me?"

_____

_____

_____

_____

_____

Now, revise/redefine them.

Tease out what the intangible, underlying philosophy is. For example, if you identified family or friends above, give thought to what is the motivating need behind it. For instance, is it love and connection, or filling a void?

_____

_____

_____

> **EXERCISE 2.2   GUIDING PRINCIPLES**
>
> What guiding principle(s) define(s) you? [Ex.: be happy, give happiness, honor the Divine Light in everyone, etc.]
>
> _____
>
> _____
>
> _____

Spirit gives us life. It is our animating philosophy of how the world works. We have evolved from formless, unshaped babies into sentient beings. Before we developed our own animating philosophy, we adopted that of those around us. As we grew, perceptions and misperceptions accumulated to shape and reshape it. As we grew through the developmental stages, we began to define ourselves as "I", going through the famous "mine" stage. We developed a sense of identity, and something began to develop that we call the ego.

THE EGO IS GREAT

We need the ego to protect us from pain, promote pleasure and help us achieve our goals. But it needs to be tamed and disciplined (no, this is not a lesson in shoulda-woulda-coulda). The ego observes the world and figures out how it all works in order to protect the self. Ego translates into a pattern of thinking as we grow. It has served to physically protect us as it formulated theories about the world. For instance, a tiger in your living room is danger. Danger is a threat, so RUN! Not a bad idea when faced with a tiger. The ego has done this so well that when our bodies perceive any threat to our mental, emotional or spiritual self, the "fight-or-flight" mechanism is triggered. Add to this that our bodies will at times overinterpret threats, and we have problems. An example of this is road rage. Sure, traffic is dangerous (a 1½ tons of steel bearing down on you can be pretty threatening), but we have instituted rules to control the threat of traffic. Despite the rules, our bodies will react. The fight-or-flight reaction is not a safe way to blow off steam/negative energy in traffic (flipping someone the finger or engaging in other exhibitions of road rage are not safe or mature ways of dealing with stress).

The ego further assimilated rights and wrongs and how the world should work as we grew and matured. Misperceptions were formed when we saw and interpreted many ideas through the eyes of a child. The ego observed both threats and solutions on this juvenile level. We heard from our parents or others, who instilled in us concepts such as "People are out to get you," "They're only out for themselves" and "Life is tough, then you die." Along the way, traumatic events can arrest the ego's growth at any stage, resulting in childish behavior as a matter of form. Or perhaps when under stress we may revert to that child, behaving and reacting childishly. Again, the ego is defending and protecting the self and what is "mine." A common example of this is when we try something that we feel self-conscious about. We hear laughter. We assume it is someone laughing at us. We withdraw and sulk or get angry and lash out. Our adult self can look at this and realize that 99 percent of what happens around us has nothing to do with us — including that laughter.

The emotional reactions of anger, fear and frustration that we experience are the juvenile ego reacting to the world. Recognizing this, acknowledging the pain and giving yourself comfort, gives you a new perspective, a new awareness of self.

Among other things, gang members have assimilated edicts such as, "They're out to get you" and "Take care of your own" to an extreme degree, with very specific definitions of who "they" and "we" are. But all of us have assimilated these to varying degrees, and they can kick-in in times of stress, all in the name of protecting the self and what is mine.

Other time-honored words of wisdom or scripts that the ego may have assimilated can be just as destructive:

> » Happily ever after… you've got to find **it**, find someone and **it** will all work out.
> » **It** shouldn't be this hard, why me – **I** am a victim…**THEY** are out to get **me.**
> » I'd better act quick and take what **I** can get, otherwise **I** am the victim.

- » "There's a reason why they call it WORK, **it's** not meant to be fun [or rewarding….]."
- » Even seemingly positive ones: "Find yourself a nice white-collar job and **they'll** take care of you" can set you up for disappointment.
- » What are some of yours?
- » _____
- » _____
- » _____
- » _____

Words are extremely powerful tools. When they are formulated, into catchy phrases like these, they can frame reality, making it possible to repeat and reinforce the same thought. Before long, they are words of wisdom, framing generations.

EVERYTHING IS ENERGY

Einstein theorized that everything is energy. I was watching NOVA a few years ago, a program looking at Eintein's theory, and I remembered back to my high school biology class. Why the teacher was talking physics I don't know, but I do remember our discussion about that black speckled countertop that functioned both as his desk and as a surface for experiments. The table is made up of atoms. Atoms as we know are in constant motion, with their electrons and protons swapping places whenever they get bored (I teach physics in my other life). Some substances are inherently more active and volatile, but even the atoms in this countertop were in constant motion. NOVA was reporting that it has now been discovered that the atom is made of even smaller particles called quanta, which are sheer energy.

OK. That's enough of the physics lesson. Almost. The human body is energy as well. I love Henry Grayson's description: "Our bodies… are composed of 99.999 percent 'dancing energy', where subatomic particles are popping in and out of existence moment by moment." Additionally, it has now been shown with Krilian photographs that energy fields emanate from everyone. Haven't we known this for a long, long time? Even in colloquial language when we say someone is spirited, it means they have a lot of energy.

To illustrate this, imagine the following: you are at the end of a very long day, you missed a deadline, you missed lunch, your employees were disgruntled about new changes in the benefits package, you spilled coffee down your white shirt before an important meeting, and to top it all, someone flipped you the bird in traffic on the way home. There you are with jangled nerves, tired, hungry and irritable. Now, raise your right hand. Make it quiver, keeping your elbow steady. Picture yourself as this quivering, upraised hand. You come home, where everyone else had a great day (raise your left hand and picture your family as this hand, upraised but relaxed and still). You immediately begin to download your negative energy. Before long, the whole family is feeling your frustration, and this energy starts getting passed back and forth, as both parties start the "Isn't it terrible" mantra. Imagine the hands swapping this energy back and forth, and it is not long before both hands are continuously quivering with frustrated energy. The energy of your day has now affected everyone in the family. I call this the swap-um effect. It is a globalized feeling of victimization, where you are triangulating (involving a third party) and displacing the energy in an effort to cope.

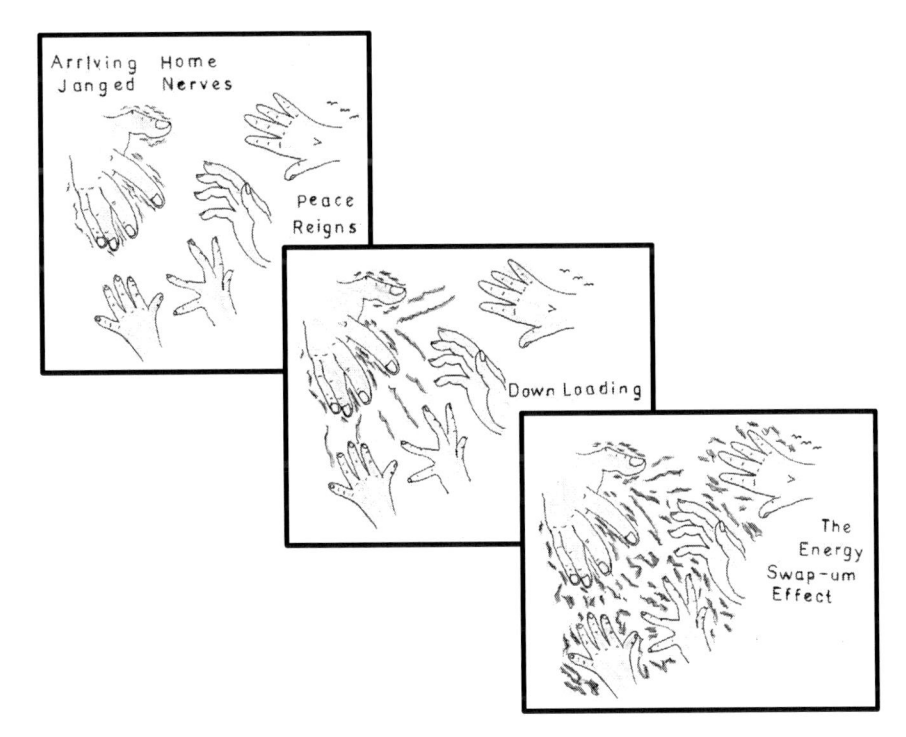

This is learned behavior. Isn't this what one does at the end of the day? Download so you can enjoy your evening? It works, doesn't it? You got it off your chest. No -- it didn't work to restore peace and balance. You may feel somewhat better, but you have passed off the energy to others in your environment. There are better ways than reliving it, than swapping the negative energy back and forth.

Everything is energy. It is not really a quantum leap to recognize that we influence our surroundings -- that we affect others in both positive and negative ways. It is even conceivable that we can actively participate in the creation of our surroundings and our relationships. We can, in fact, affect everything in our lives, from how a meeting proceeds to the ambiance of our homes and families at the end of a very long and difficult day.

> Every thought is prayer.

Even thought is energy, and no thought is idle. Our thoughts are "a powerful creative force extending from our bodies, out to others and the universe, affecting every aspect of our lives, and relationships" (*Mindful Loving*). You are participating in creation. You have the power as a sentient adult to think carefully and reevaluate your animating philosophy (Exercises 2.1 and 2.2). We can no longer consider ourselves separate, powerless victims. You can change your thoughts and create your own reality.

So, be careful what you think about

Just imagine. What could our world look like if everyone truly believed this and used their power, their energy to "continually create peace and joy in every relationship?" Now THERE is a thought.

The power of thought...

A fascinating tie-in here is that in the New Testament, John 1:1-2 states: "In the beginning was the Word, and the Word was with God, and the Word was God." Even the WORD began as thought, even Creation began as thought, and because God is love, that thought was love.

SECTION II

21ST CENTURY TOOLS

> **We need a holistic approach to living well**

OF SPECIAL NOTE......

So far, we have explored what living well looks like. We have found that despite all the findings of science and the progress of technology, the main skill needed to live well is love. For most of us this does not mean going around throwing flower petals saying, "Peace, love, joy." So the question becomes: How do we put love into action? How can we incorporate this into our personal lifestyles? What does the practice of love look like in the 21st century?

As we explore our options, let us consider the wisdom from spiritual communities. According to The Tao Te Ching, the tools for living well are balance, simplicity and harmony. Christianity tells us the tools are faith, hope and charity (loving kindness) (I Corinthians 13:13). In Buddhism, it is about mindfulness. And according to *A Course In Miracles* (Lesson 190, v. 11:2), just do it, just choose it. "We are free to choose our joy instead of pain" And "...it is you who have the power to dominate all things you see by merely recognizing what you are [the embodiment of love]" (Lesson 190, v.5:7). All are similar concepts; none are mutually exclusive.

What is also clear is that we, as a community of people, are not living well. We are not consistently applying our coping strategies in the presence of 21st century abundance and our long life expectancy. We excel at addictive behaviors and addictive relationships, typically because we have been looking outside of ourselves for answers and satisfaction. The time is now too look inward to learn to flex what Brian Luke Seaward calls our spiritual muscles: "...humor, optimism, patience, compassion, courage, curiosity, humbleness, forgiveness, faith, creativity, persistence, confidence and love. These are our divine inner resources. We need new challenges in order for them to remain effective... to flex and stretch them, moving them against resistance in order to grow. We fine tune-them with each new challenge." (*Stressed is Desserts Spelled Backwards*)

It was Aristotle who introduced the concept of holism, saying,

"The whole is more than the sum of its parts." The old saying "All work and no play makes Jack a dull boy" is less eloquent but more to the point. It succinctly points out that when an area of our life is out of balance, it is like driving with a flat tire. If we look at our lives holistically, we can keep life in balance. When riding on the rim, how well will we navigate speed bumps? We feel every jolt. Most of us know that we could eat healthier, get more aerobic exercise, spend more time with ourselves and our families, spend more time outdoors and at play and less time at work. Knowing this, why are we not doing it?

It is those nasty gremlins and boggarts (Ex. 1.3) again. At the top of the list is that old monkey on our back -- time. Where is the time? Where is the energy? My own experience with physical exercise illustrates what a fair-weather friend time can be. When my schedule was Monday through Friday, 8-5 (and beyond) with teaching and engagements, being a single mom, etc., etc., finding time was a chore. The excuses were profuse. And many of them were valid: "I'm tired; my schedule is so chaotic, I can't get a routine going; I'm on my feet all day...surely that counts as exercise." And the excuses went on. No matter how valid my excuses were, these yah-buts were still not lowering my blood pressure or my cholesterol. The time monkey is a real entity. It was not until I made a concerted effort, giving it priority, that I was able to get myself together and actually exercise -- actually make it a habit and find out what did and did not work for me.

Now is the time to leave the yah-buts at the door. As you move through the book, if you find yourself hesitating, spend some time identifying why. What is standing in your way? What is scary about this? Does it have to do with how your significant other will react to these changes? Is it the work involved? You may need to seriously evaluate the validity of these barriers. Journaling is an excellent method of analyzing patterns and behaviors. Sometimes it is enough to vent your yah-buts -- to see either how irrelevant they are, or to help you make a conscious choice about priorities and what *you* want.

Below is the Yah-But Exercise. Each time you work through it, put the result on an index card and display it in a prominent place for yourself. This will help focus your thoughts, clarify your values and devise a strategic plan.

EXERCISE 3.1   THE YAH-BUT EXERCISE

Compile a list of changes that you would like to make in your life and what's keeping you from realizing them.

Example: I'd like to spend more time with my family, *but* I travel a lot for my job.

Now, exchange "and" every time you wrote "but". See how that changes the statement, moving from excuse-making into problem-solving mode.

It now reads: I'd like to spend more time with my family, and I travel a lot for my job… **so** I need to find ways to bring my family along during some of my travels.

Post your new statements in prominent places, allowing your subconscious right brain to keep working through it.

Adapted from: D. Pink: *A Whole New Mind*

See also, Ex. 6.4

Chapter 3
THE POWER OF WORDS

> You become that which you think about.
> *Don Coyhis*

A number of years ago, I had the honor of hearing Don Coyhis speak. As a member of the Mohican Nation, he brought to the corporate community the teachings of the Medicine Wheel. He spoke this simple truth that has resonated with me ever since: "You become that which you think about."

Words shape our thoughts and give them energy. Positive or negative, they can frame our reality and even create that reality. As thoughts, they produce energy, and when we speak or write them, we breathe life into them. What kind of energy is involved when someone asks, "How are you doing?" and you respond with, "I'm doing," as opposed to responding, "I'm great, thanks for asking. How are you?" or even "I have a number of challenges on my plate today, but it's going to be great." Or more simply: "I'm great!" Feel the difference to your spirit.

Venting has a place in helping us cope, but overuse of it can be addictive and tends to reinforce the victim role. Simon and Simon, in their book *Forgiveness,* observe: "the negative things you say to yourself usually make old wounds hurt more." So limit that sort of negativity. Practice self-control. Move on and create peace and joy

THE POWER OF POSITIVE THINKING

Everything begins as a thought.

According to the Judeo-Christian tradition, it all began with God saying, "Let there be light." But before He said these famous words, He had to have a vision, then a thought. Words preceded the deed. And so it has been since the dawn of time. The Gospel of John states "In the beginning was the WORD." The Buddha said "With our thoughts we make our world."

Psychologists have estimated that we have 60,000 thoughts every day. Wow. Not all of them are as profound as the ones that created the galaxy, and 90 - 95 percent of them are, in fact, repetitions, common thought patterns, themes that we repeat and dwell on, sometimes for years. "The nature of ego's thinking [is such that] we may find ourselves constantly thinking, judging, analyzing, criticizing, projecting, reliving, or even rehearsing conversations in our minds. Sometimes these negative voices in our heads are so pervasive that if we ever seem to have a modicum of peace at all, it is temporary and easily displaced." (*Mindful Loving*) At times these "enemy thoughts" based on ego thinking, seem to be bent on cutting up our serenity and destroying our happiness. It is a misguided, outdated attempt to protect the self.

When we recognize this, we can begin to isolate, identify and choose what we want to think about. We can choose thoughts of fear -- and with it, anxiety, anger, pain, hatred and the sure-enough principle. Or we can choose thoughts of love -- and along with it, peace, joy and happiness.

The Sure Enough Principle

The power of thought…we are co-creators in our reality.

- - - - -

You believe or think something will happen, such as "It's going to be a tough day, there's a lot to do and a big meeting as well." Sure enough, you have a flat tire on the way to work, you're late for the meeting, you're harried and flustered and forget one of your key points.

Don Coyhis

It is a common assumption that our thoughts are private and influence our experience only if we act upon them. If this were so, how is it that dogs can smell fear? Even when our voice wheedles and cajoles, never wavering with nervousness, they can still smell the fear. At its most basic level, a thought is energy. Synapses are firing as the thought moves around our brains, being considered from every angle. Fear hormones are released (preparing us for fight or flight), and this is what the animal senses. "Every so-called idle thought is actually a powerful creative force extending out from our bodies, to others and to the universe, affecting every aspect of our lives and relationships." (Mindful Loving).

THE ART OF POSITIVE THINKING

Knowing that words are powerful tools, I started playing with them.

One way to define myself would be by my abilities, limitations and liabilities:

> I am a nurse/teacher/weaver.
> I am single/married/divorced.
> I am a parent/I am childless.
> I am in debt/wealthy.
> I am ill.
> I am a victim.

But I have a choice -- instead of using these ego definitions of self, I could instead say….

I am.

Try defining yourself this way. Say out loud: I am.

Can you feel the freedom, the limitlessness of it? Do you feel the awe?

Here, in this space where **I am:**

> **I am happiness.**
> **I am light.**
> **I am love.**
> **I am the divine.**
> **I am.**

Note how **I am** is incompatible with the concept "I am a victim" or "I am my debt."

Many world religions and philosophies support the thought that you are the light of the world, a child of God and thereby divine by birthright. In Christianity, there is a profound play on words with this construct. God defined himself as "I AM;" Jesus told us that God is love and that we are children of God. So if you literally do the math, you come up with "I am love" -- we are all divine.

> Note: As I was editing this section of the book, I was printing out these pages on recycled quizzes that my nursing students had given to fifth graders. One of the fifth graders had written on the back side of the quiz, big and bold "**I'm Awesome**." What fun! It's nice to believe that there are no coincidences. We all need to take a lesson from this fifth grader -- this is what we all need to be saying to ourselves.

POSITIVE AFFIRMATIONS VERSUS AWFULIZING

Every thought is an affirmation, whether positive or negative. Every moment of every day we can choose a positive or negative attitude and positive or negative affirmations. We can also actively replace negative affirmations with positive ones, thereby creating our own reality through the vibes we give off, affecting our surroundings. We can actively attract positive or negative things in our life through our thinking. Poverty thinking will beget a life of poverty. Poverty thinking is the opposite of the Enoughness Principle. The Enoughness Principle says there is enough love, happiness, beauty and even material things for everyone, including you. (Read more about the Enoughness Principle in Chapter 6.)

One form of negative affirmations is "awfulizing." It creates a mind rut, mud-mind and stinkin'-thinkin' mode of operation. To awfulize is to make a situation out to be worse than it really is; to complain and exaggerate the severity. It is characterizing a mundane issue as some horrible, catastrophic occurrence and to project horrible outcomes that have not yet happened (Hebert). In other words, to make the proverbial mountain out of a molehill, and to allow the self-fulfilling prophecy (AKA: the Law of Attraction or Power of Intention) to manifest itself.

The following exercises are tried-and-true methods to break through the awfulizing mode we get ourselves in. I have used all of them many times, always to good effect.

Visit the Vital Affirmations website sometime. They give many concrete examples of positive affirmations on everything from weight loss to romance to abundance. They also speak of techniques for supercharging your affirmations, some of which I've already mentioned:

- Affirmation mirror work: look yourself straight in the eye while saying them.
- Written affirmations: write them many times, leave them on cards in various places.
- Say your affirmations with passion -- the higher your emotional state as you say them, the more effective they are.
- Sing or chant affirmations

So, in your thinking, remember:

- The power of thought affects your life and others around you.
- You become that which you think about.
  - Think on gratitude and you will have blessings.
  - Think on love and you will be loved.

EXERCISE 3.2 AN ATTITUDE OF GRATITUDE

On a notecard, write down everything that you are grateful for. Add to it as you think of more. Keep this card with you to add to or to cheer you whenever you are feeling low.

- Keep this next to your bed to review and add to every night and morning
- Have several and post them in prominent places for you to see throughout the day.

> **EXERCISE 3.3 REFOCUS TOOLS FOR STINKIN'-THINKIN'/MUD-MIND TIMES**
>
> Write down phrases from a song, poem, prayer, etc. Have several to choose from for various times or situations. When you slip into a mind rut, sing or repeat the phrase until you can snap out of it or otherwise distract yourself. This is one of my favorite tools.
>
> _____
>
> _____
>
> _____

CHANGE YOUR THOUGHTS

Be patient with yourself. Whenever you feel or observe the first signs of negative thoughts, pull out your Gratitude cards or Magical Moments/Happy Thoughts Cards (Ex. 3.4), or your refocus song and deliberately think positive thoughts. They will help you refocus on what you truly want in your life. You become that which you think about. Find a quote that you like and keep it in your pocket or in strategic places -- dashboard of car, bedroom mirror or your computer monitor -- whatever works for you. I have different quotes in all these places. I have "Every Breath is Prayer" on my bedroom mirror; "The future belongs to those who believe in the beauty of their dreams" (Eleanor Roosevelt) sits in front of my computer; and The Prayer of St. Francis is on my car dashboard "Lord, make me an instrument of thy peace". Song is a powerful tool, also. You have not only the words, which appeal to the left brain in all of us, but the music, which permeates the right brain as well. These can help empty the mind, becoming a moment of meditation, a clearing of the fog, a washing away of the mud.

Exercise 3.4 Magical Moments -- The Happy Thoughts Card

This one is slightly different from the Attitude of Gratitude exercise. You can combine them if you wish, but again, on an index card, write down special moments in your life. I call them magic moments.

For example: one Friday evening when my only child was in high school, I sat at home, reading, while her friends, who could now drive, had taken her to the football game. I wasn't invited. I could have invited myself, but I really don't care to sit on cold bleachers watching boys run up and down in the mud and tackling each other. I was perhaps even relishing those first twangs of empty nest, wondering vaguely if I should be looking for something to do on a Friday evening. I didn't. I sat there wallowing. My daughter came home at about 11 p.m., sat down on a stool in the living room across from me and started chattering. She must have gone on for a full 15 to 20 minutes, non-stop. This is the child who has been monosyllabic since birth. When asked what she did with her day or what she's thinking, I always felt myself lucky to get a "Fine" or "OK" out of the deal. Yet, here we were, 20 minutes of non-stop bubbling.

What a treasure. What a moment. If I had rushed out and found something to fill this "void," this moment would never have happened for us.

In Burma, a parable about gourds states that a gourd's value and usefulness as a bowl is in its emptiness (D. Gilman: *Incident at Badyama*).

Now, I have only to think the phrase "magic moments," and all the joy and contentment of that moment is present with me.

Continued on next page...

EXERCISE 3.4   MAGICAL MOMENTS (CONTINUED)

What are your magical moments?

_____
_____
_____
_____
_____
_____

Add to your list of magical moments as you think of more. Keep this card with you to add to or to cheer you whenever you are feeling low.

EXERCISE 3.5   HOW TO CREATE AFFIRMATIONS

Look back at Be a Swan, Exercise 1.2. List the most important issues.

_____
_____
_____
_____

Now look at each item on the list and write out a few positive statements for each. They must be positive and in the present tense -- focus on what you **do** want, **not** on what you do not want.

Continued on next page...

EXERCISE 3.5   HOW TO CREATE AFFIRMATIONS (CONTINUED)

For example, my list of things that are important to me includes "a fulfilling job."

My affirmation might look like this

"I have a wonderful job that fulfills me on many levels."

Even if my job were not fulfilling, this affirmation would plant a seed that will fulfill itself.

Creating your affirmations is the perfect way to get the right affirmations for you. Below are a few more examples. These should give you a good idea of how affirmations should look and feel. Some affirmations are called releasing affirmations. For example: "I am ready and willing to release the past, now."

Additional affirmations:

- Every cell in my body vibrates with energy and health.
- Loving myself heals my life. I nourish my mind, body and soul.
- My body heals quickly and easily.
- I prosper wherever I turn, and I know that I deserve prosperity of all kinds.
- The more grateful I am, the more reasons I find to be grateful.
- I give out love, and it is returned to me multiplied.
- I attract only healthy relationships.
- When I believe in myself, so do others.
- I am my unique self -- special, creative and wonderful.
- I am at peace.
- Life is a joy filled with delightful surprises.
- I choose love, joy and freedom, open my heart and allow wonderful things to flow into my life.

Adapted from Positive Affirmations http://www.vitalaffirmations.com at The Positive Mindset Website

THE ART OF JOURNALING

Many advocates of journaling recommend writing daily, if only for five minutes. I had previously used my journal to pour out my heart on high emotional issues (happy, sad, upset), knowing that in writing it out I could work through the issues to a clearer mind. I am now attempting to use it more often for reflecting on the multiple spiritual issues that surround me every day. I'm still new at this and flounder, at times, but willing to work it.

According to Brian Luke Seaward, journal writing initiates communication between the mind and the soul through self-reflection. This is a necessary first step in the resolution and closure of perceived stress. It is a mode of catharsis through which to express the full range of emotions. Research demonstrates that those who journal using self-reflection to uncover feelings rather than address superficial topics have heightened immune systems, decreased cholesterol levels, decreased stress levels, and increased coping abilities. Journaling has even been found to lower elevated blood pressure.

The reason for this effect becomes intuitively obvious when you consider that the emotions that you are experiencing are the result of the fight-or-flight response, activated by the perceived threat, hurt, injustice, etc. Your body has released a "stress cocktail" of hormones, ready for fight or flight. All this pent-up energy is ready for action, but there is nowhere to go. Exercise is a wonderful outlet for this built up energy. So is journaling. With journaling, you are getting it out, releasing it in a constructive fashion instead of letting that energy turn inward, causing stress and disease (dis-ease).

Poetry and letter writing can also foster similar results. The discipline of rhyme can make order out of chaos. Letter writing can focus the attention or allow the telling of events in a story-telling modality. The act of releasing the thoughts and feelings onto paper is similar to Professor Dumbledore's pensieve in the book *Harry Potter and the Goblet of Fire*. "I sometimes find ...that I simply have too many thoughts and memories crammed into my mind....at these times, I use the Pensieve. One simply siphons the excess thoughts from one's mind, pours them into the basin, and examines them at one's leisure. It becomes easier to spot patterns and links... when they are in this form." J. K. Rowling's analogy is simply brilliant.

> "I find I've worried about a lot of things, most of which never happened."
>
> *Mark Twain*

The Pensieve

Wouldn't it be wonderful if it was as easy to get rid of mud mind as using the pensieve in the Harry Potter books? The pensieve is a shallow stone basin, carved with runes and symbols. Professor Dumbledore uses the pensieve to *"siphon excess thoughts from one's mind, pouring them into the basin, and examining them at one's leisure. It becomes easier to spot patterns and links... when they are in this form."* It allows a cool, objective mind to observe and analyze.

In *Change Your Mind, Change Your Life,* Jampolski and Cirincione liken relationships to laboratories "where we can discover what unconditional love is all about...[It is an] opportunity to learn how to heal the illusion of separation and to experience all hearts and minds as one;" how to transform fear, guilt, judgment] and blame into love. Relationships, no matter how fleeting or insignificant, provide us with opportunities to learn and grow. Practice capturing them in the written word.

Exercise 3.6 So Write Already!
Journaling tips...pick which ones work for you

1. Have a notebook devoted just to journal writing and a pen or pencil.
2. Sometimes you may want to start with a list of the things going through your head. Then when you write, write free-flowing prose without stopping or editing for punctuation or spelling.
3. Play some relaxing background music (instrumental, classical or new age, etc.).
4. Consider holding a shell or tumbled stone.
5. Consider writing poetry, writing a letter, leaving space for doodles, drawings and photos.
6. Be sure to include both stressful events and positive experiences.
7. Find a private place to write, and keep your journal private so you can feel free to write uncensored.
8. Try to write for a minimum of 15 to 20 minutes (or a minimum of three pages) about three times per week.
9. Do it for fun! Sometimes choose to write on a personal goal or about something that fascinates you.
10. Consider writing a daily note in a joy journal. Loretta LaRoche suggests that, at bedtime, you write down three kind things that were done for you and three kind things you did for someone else today. Or just three things that delighted you today. She has 24 additional ideas for your joy journal, including writing down ways you could surprise and delight someone you love and things you are grateful for.

THE ART OF COMMUNICATION

> [Communication] cannot be banked. There must be a continuous, mutual and reciprocal support of personal worth in a love relationship [for healthy maintenance of the relationship].
>
> <u>The Secret of Staying in Love</u>, John Powell, S.J.

Timely communication: Even when stressed -- especially when stressed -- we need to communicate on a timely basis. Timing is a matter of balance that needs to be learned. Sometimes time and space are needed to take the heat out of an argument so we can come back to it fresh. Conversely, if too much time passes details are forgotten, resulting in a flat conversation. But there is no place in a healthy relationship for withholding or not being up front.

Anything worth having -- job, college education -- is worth a bit of work. And yes, relationships can be work at times, but the payoff can be without bounds. You might argue that you have been communicating all of your life. But what avid fisherman wouldn't put in the work to learn a new technique, given a chance to be taught a fool-proof way to catch "the big one?"

Communication continually challenges us. While everything is going well, communication is easy. But patterns we learned growing up may not be the basis for long-term healthy relationships in new situations, or when we are under stress. Stress gives us tunnel vision (our peripheral vision literally narrows when we are under stress) and we tend to hear what we want or expect to hear.

Always remember several critical aspects of communication:

(1) Communication is listening. It is probably 10 percent message (you already know the message you want to send) and 90 percent feedback, i.e., are you listening?
(1) Communication cannot be banked -- it must be continuous and mutual.

According to John Powell, in his book *The Secret of Staying in Love*, there are two levels of communication: discussion and dialogue.

(1) Discussion is informational in nature. It is the sharing of thoughts, values, making plans or decisions together. It is predominantly intellectual in nature.
(1) Dialogue, on the other hand, is the sharing of emotions or feelings. It is "easier to discuss a problem, harder to expose a feeling."

A COMMUNICATION EXAMPLE

The following is a fairly mundane conversation, but see if you can pick out what was done right and what was done poorly.

Fred, talking about his latest finds in his ancestry search, pronounced Yorkshire as York-shy-er.

I playfully interject, "It's Yorksure."
F: "It doesn't matter. "
Me, being playful: "Yes it does, it's Yorksure."
F: "You're not interested in this," and he clams up.
Me, protesting: "I am. What's this all about?
What are you upset about? I was being playful."
F: "It didn't sound that way."
Me: "But it was."
F: "OK, I don't want to talk about it anymore."
Me: "You don't sound like you believe me, that I was being playful."
F: "It came across sarcastic."
Me: "How long have you known me? I was being playful. Why don't you believe me?"
F: "I would if your words and behavior were more in line."
Me: "I said I was sorry."
F: "No you didn't."
Me: "I'm sure I did, I said I was just being playful."
F: "I didn't hear it."

I was very upset, struggling with his spoken desire not to talk about it anymore and my knowledge that we needed to sort this out. We could not sweep this under the rug, because it would only fester.

Fred spoke first: "It doesn't feel safe when you say something like that. I don't feel like sharing something I'm excited about. I switch to safer topics."

Ah-hah. Communication really starts now.

Points of interest:

- » Do you see where he expected and did not hear an apology?
- » I thought my genuine protests that "it was playful" were an apology.
- » The situation deescalated with the use of "I feel…."
- » Do you see how I thought I had clearly communicated?
- » I had also let ego step in when I presumed it was a matter of trust, not just mis-communication. What I had meant as playful came across as ridicule or derision.
- » Also, both of us hung in there until a win-win resolution occurred.

Here is another point of interest, so you can see how our childhood can come into the action. Let me share an inside note. I am coming to understand that it is because I grew up with this type of teasing that I did not see it as ridicule. It is a version of the one-upmanship that was played ferociously in my family of origin. Consequently, I have trouble distinguishing between teasing, playfulness, ridicule, mocking and sarcasm. They were all labeled good-natured teasing/playfulness by my family, and when we got upset about it, we were told not to be so sensitive.

The field of neurolinguistics studies how language can shape our emotional development. Very simply, lacking the words to describe or properly label an issue, concern or feeling can affect our emotional maturity, our emotional intelligence. Because I have trouble distinguishing between teasing, ridicule, mocking and sarcasm, this is an area I need to work on, because it tends to stimulate hurt feelings out of proportion to the event.

"If I dwell on a loving thought about someone else, I feel instantly joyful. If I dwell on an angry or resentful thought, I have attacked my own inner peace and it is annihilated instantly."

Mindful Loving

EXERCISE 3.7 CONSCIOUS LISTENING

"You must practice deep looking" without judgment or comment to really understand this person. Without understanding, love is not possible. This takes time, being attentive, observant and you must look deeply. Seek understanding. "The practice of understanding is the practice of meditation"…to look deeply into the heart of things.

(Thich Nhat Hanh, True Love)

<u>Listening exercise</u>

- » With your partner, identify who is the speaker and who is the listener
- » The listener's role is just to listen, without comment or judgment
- » Start with 1 to 2 minutes of mindful breathing (Exercise 11.4).
- » Deep, attentive listening is a meditation….maintain calm.
- » Be actively compassionate.
- » Listen with calmness and understanding, always non-judgmental.
- » Just listen for an hour.
- » Then schedule your hour. Strive to do this one to two times per week.
- » The speaker describes a significant stress or issue in his/her life right now
- » Then switch roles
- » How did it make you feel to be listened to?
- » Did you fix anything? Did you have to fix anything?*

Thich Nhat Han recommends a full hour in each role. That may be too much, especially at first, so try 10 minutes initially and respect that boundary. Lengthen it when you are comfortable doing so.

*Answer: Just being listened to can be enough. It validates you and allows you to hear your own inner wisdom.

EXERCISE 3.8   THE DAILY FAMILY POWWOW

This exercise is written for family life, but I have also used this with my staff. It's been a valuable tool, making for a much better day when we do it. One of the main premises is that communication cannot wait. The best supervisor I ever had was at one of my toughest jobs. I was a supervisor in a nursing home, and I have never had a better relationship with my boss or fellow employees. My supervisor met with me and the other managers nearly every day for lunch. Timely communication happened, she knew all the issues and concerns, there were no surprises, and there was support for what we were doing as well as suggestions and feedback.

At home, you are no less a team. Team members need to communicate. What would happen to a winning football team if players stopped having their huddle? It would fall apart. Communication needs to happen at a minimum of at least once a day; better if it is at least twice a day. Not just coordinating schedules (discussion) but true dialogue, communication of emotions and feelings.

During these powwows, two key practices are necessary, according to Thich Nhat Hanh (*True Love*): You want to

Be truly *present*
(love is being there).

Recognize the presence of the other
("To love is to be,
to be loved is to be recognized by the other").

Continued on next page...

Exercise 3.8   The Daily Family Powwow (continued)

Suggestions for the daily powwow

At the beginning of the day, take two or three slow, deep breaths together to help focus on this moment in time and ask, "So, what's your schedule today?" At the very least, this may give you an inkling of the likely state your family will be in by evening, and you can plan to give them space when they get home. This practice does not allow things to fester.

Suggestions for the weekly powwow

At least once a week, have a longer powwow, perhaps as much as an hour. Formally, or informally, whatever works. Make this for just the two of you. This time is especially important when there are children or extended family members in the household. Make a habit of it before children arrive as it to grow with you and be an unbeatable strength. This is a time when you focus on conscious listening.

In a relationship, it is a way to determine how decisions are made, how chores are divvied up: trash, dishes, meals, laundry, shopping, yard work, cleaning the gutters, child care; finances. You can also use this time to review finances and goals.

Start with two or three slow deep breaths together to help focus on this moment and practice conscious listening.

------- -------- -------

Starting powwows for the first time may feel awkward. Also, they may fall to the wayside when things are going smoothly. To start them up, it can be helpful to say, "Things aren't going as smoothly as they could, let's try this new strategy (or start having powwows again) and see if we can help us out a bit."

Chapter 4
THE POWER OF SPIRITUALITY

> "Joy…is the ultimate form of prayer….It is the living affirmation of our inherent perfection…. Joy and laughter may be forms of enlightenment, involuntary moments when we are fully present."
>
> <u>The Art of Everyday Ecstasy</u>, *Margot Anand*

It is an illusion that we are separate, isolated human beings. It is an illusion that we are unlovable (something our ego tells us when we have messed up). Spirituality is not devotion to a religion or doing good; rather it is about our relationship with our Higher Power or God; it is about connectedness and love. Spirituality is a life force that gives us passion and meaning and purpose in life. It is also that sense of awe and wonder, that appreciation for the mystery of life itself.

Love is certainly one of the most important elements of spirituality. In this chapter, we will discuss characteristics of and tools for a balanced spiritual life: meditation, mindfulness and creation of a sanctuary. We will explore the power of surrender or letting go, which has some surprising implications.

But first, to put these tools to use, a quiet space, a sanctuary is called for. A place to relax and rejuvenate.

TAKE FIVE…CREATE A SANCTUARY

We are finding that our brains need downtime. Not just sleep, when our brain is still processing information, but a place where there is space between our thoughts. Have you ever been doing something and the solution to something totally unrelated just came to you? When we are looking for a solution, we typically go round and round and round, thinking that we are looking at it from different angles, but often what we are doing is reinforcing the same brain pathway and creating a mental rut. Think of the deep ruts in a now-dry muddy drive—it becomes very hard to steer out of them. When we meditate, we create space between our thoughts, allowing us to hear our own wisdom or that of our Higher Power.

Though distraction is a useful tool (TV, computer games, woodworking, quilting, etc.), it is still not giving our brains true rest. To achieve this, we can create a space where we can go to relax, unwind, meditate, regain balance and replenish our energies. A space away from the noise and lure of TV and other distractions; a place I call sanctuary. It can be as small as a corner of your bedroom or your porch swing and still be effective. A sanctuary is a sacred place set apart, dedicated exclusively to a single use, worthy of reverence and respect…where a person's house is his castle, dedicated to the nurturing and rejuvenation of the spirit.

Without this space, for both our families and for ourselves, we get GIGO (garbage in garbage out). A whole body of science explores color and design and its influence on the psyche, so in your creation of this space, so you will even want to consider the selection of furnishings, color and knick-knacks -- or lack of -- simplicity is another desired feature for this space.

In creating my family's sanctuary, I have never allowed the television in the bedrooms. The bedroom has always been a retreat. Recently I was able to create a space there that feels like a cocoon. By the time my daughter moved home in the middle of college to finish her education by commuting, I had had 1½ years of space and time on my own. We moved furniture around to accommodate a second adult in my small space, and I took a spare lazy-boy chair and tucked it into a corner of my bedroom. I can see the tops of the trees through the window and I have space for a table or two next to it. It is my space, my retreat. At the end of a long day, before I gear myself up for dinner, I spend time here, unwinding. Extending this concept throughout my home leads to careful selection of TV programs, news, movies, music.

I have come to treasure this space so much that wherever I go I create a sanctuary, even if it is to go outside for five minutes on lunch break, or take five at the office with the door closed. My goal would be to be able to tune in to that sanctuary wherever I am. There are times when I can tune it in, when I remember to be an observer and not react. I use the "Every breath is prayer" mantra and tune out the world, but at times, I flounder. I still need a physical space. My sanctuary -- the little corner in my bedroom.

    We must give attention to the divine and the purpose of life, and sanctuary is where we can find it. Find a space. Create a space. Use and protect that space.

EXERCISE 4.1   CREATING A SANCTUARY

Define for yourself what your sanctuary needs to look like, where is it, how is it furnished? describe the use of nature, music, candles and absence of electronics. (See also Ex. 13.1.)

_____

_____

_____

_____

_____

The Power of Meditation

    A quiet mind. There is so much running through our heads that we often cannot hear our own wisdom when we try. In the movie "*August Rush*," the musician/composer said, "The music is always playing; sometimes I get to hear it."

    Kamal Sarma diagrams it well… before and after meditation

    To truly *listen*, it would behoove us to clear our minds first. Those 60,000 thoughts running around in there every day need periodically to be put to rest. While sleeping, vacationing or reading a book, our minds are still processing. Perhaps we feel as if we shut it off when we zone out in front of the boob tube, but we are just filling it with someone else's interpretations and ideas. By giving it a real rest through meditation, we are allowing our minds to get food and oxygen while simultaneously exercising different brain "muscles" and releasing stress. Then, the next time we take the issue up, we have a fresh perspective -- we have allowed the neural pathways to get out of that rut, to resurface or heal it.

Early in a friend's college career, he sought out a counselor's assistance because he had always had a mild case of test anxiety. He wanted to be a nurse, so he needed to overcome this to get the GPA he needed. The counselor told him that he had a mild form of obsessive-compulsive disorder (OCD) -- that he obsessed over certain issues relating to grades, studying and study habits even when time had proven that he really did not need to.

Don't we all tend to do this? Do we really have to put a label on these milder manifestations, or can we simply learn and teach effective tools to control this urge of the ego to create a mind rut? The term "mind rut" is an amazingly appropriate one when you think about how the neurons operate. When we're in a mind rut, the same set of neurons are engaged in racing around and around and around, creating an embedded pathway, making creative thought difficult.

Often it is only one thought, or one set of thoughts, that we are allowing to crowd out all others. How can we remaster our thoughts and our lives? It takes some effort, and for many of us, some new techniques. I especially like the words in Peter Cetera's song: "If I'm very still, I will hear one clear voice." Meditation recharges your senses: your sense of purpose, sense of awe, sense of connectedness and Oneness, and your sense of inner peace.

The many types of meditation fall into two distinct categories: exclusive mediation and inclusive meditation. Both promote relaxation and insights. It is a matter of finding what works for you and what you are comfortable with, and what resources, time and interest you have.

TYPES OF MEDITATION

Exclusive Meditation	Inclusive Meditation
Focusing on one object, excluding all other thoughts to increase self-awareness and promote relaxation.	*Allowing the mind to wander, you have awareness of your thoughts without judgment or emotional evaluation. You are an observer of your thoughts, practicing detached observation.*
Mental repetition -- uses a mantra such as "OM" or a short positive phrase.	Mindful eating.
Transcendental meditation (TM) -- A technique to become aware of the source behind your thoughts, awareness. A silent and peaceful level of consciousness.	Walking meditation (can be used as an exclusive mediation technique as well).
Visual concentration, steady gazing or tratak, is focusing on an object (candle flame, mandala, shell, flower) about 60 seconds without blinking. Then close your eyes and visualize the object. Repeat as needed.	Walking a labyrinth (can be used as an exclusive meditation technique as well).
Nadam, or repeated sounds, such as drums, waterfall, rolling thunder.	Zen meditation – ancient form of meditation that allows the mind to relax and experience peace.
Physical repetition – walking, swimming, weaving, gardening, tai chi.	Meditative prayer – objective contemplation of a problem with an attitude of letting go.
Tactile repetition – rosary beads or a mala (a strand of beads).	

Continued on next page...

TYPES OF MEDITATION (CONTINUED)

Meditative prayer – example: mindful contemplation of God's creation, praising God, reading Psalms.	
Tai chi – a moving meditation, where you focus on the form and breathing, allowing the mind to rest.	

Prayer can be a form of meditation. For much of my life, prayers had always seemed to be words for me: pouring out heartache, asking for guidance and wisdom, then AMEN. Never pausing to listen. But I discovered there is also meditative or contemplative prayer, a state of listening.

"Through meditation we learn to notice, acknowledge, label, and accept all of our emotions. As we become aware, we can stop carrying around what is no longer useful to us, and in letting such things go, we feel lighter and happier, and become easier to be around" (*Mental Resilience*, Kamal Sarma).

Granted, not every moment is a moment for quiet peace and joy. Action is called for at times "a time for every purpose under heaven". But the more we practice, the more we will build our repertoire for being able to *act* from a place of peace and clarity, act as we would truly want to *act*, not just knee-jerk *reacting* based on old scripts.

Have you ever seen a glass of cloudy water? When it is allowed to sit still and all the particulates and air bubbles settle, it becomes clearer. Meditation is like that. When all those 60,000 thoughts become jammed up in our heads with all the emotions that they engender, meditation calms the mind and quiets the mental noise.

I teach tai chi, and when we practice indoors because of the weather, I will often have music playing. After a few minutes of practice, I always turn the volume down. As we sink into our moving meditation, the noise in our brains quiets and the music becomes very loud.

The Power of the Mental Rut

One day as a school nurse, I had a 7-year-old who came into the clinic in tears several times, over the course of the morning. She had been crying all day in the classroom. Tummy OK, no fever, no cough, slept OK, everyone at home treating her OK, but a little boy threw up yesterday in class. She began to feel better as I talked to her. The tears dried up. She sat in the office for a little bit and I suggested she was ready to go back to her classroom. Great, silent tears started rolling down her face again. "Why are you so sad today?"

Student: 'That boy threw up in class yesterday...I can't stop thinking about it."

ME: "If you go back to class, there are lots of things to do so you don't have to think about it, you'll forget about it."

Mind rut -- all she could think about was the picture of that boy throwing up. Sounds like something I want to keep thinking about!

EXERCISE 4.2   SMILE MEDITATION

Meditate by simply sitting and smiling.
"Smile in your liver!"

<u>Eat, Pray, Love</u>, Elizabeth Gilbert

Smile at everything you see.

Note: When we smile, that particular movement of our facial muscles releases endorphins…and you're happy.

EXERCISE 4.3   THE EAGLE MEDITATION

At a pivotal point in a Native American's life (often before puberty), a youth will go on a Vision Quest. It is a rite of passage, a time alone, often in the wilderness. When he returns, he may change his name, a name often taken from animals.

Native Americans say, "To learn from an animal, you have to feel him in your muscles and bones"

When under stress, we can learn a lot from the eagle.

Practice the following meditation a couple of times. I have a notecard with just the words "Eagle Meditation" on top of my alarm clock and next to my reading chair. I use it regularly and in times of stress.

-----   -----

- » To begin this exercise, first focus your awareness on your breathing:
- » Feel the air come into your nose or mouth, and travel deep into your lungs.
  - As you inhale, feel the cooling of your nostrils. As you exhale, feel the warming of your nostrils.

Continued on next page...

> **EXERCISE 4.3 THE EAGLE MEDITATION (CONTINUED)**
>
> » Feel your stomach extend out as you inhale, then collapse as you exhale.
>   - Continue this abdominal breathing throughout. This is the relaxed breathing of sleep -- fools your body into thinking it is relaxed.
> » As you repeat this cycle of slow, deep breathing, become aware of how relaxed your body is with *each* exhalation.
> » Now, take a very slow, deep breath, as slow and as deep as you comfortably can.
> » Comfortably slow, comfortably deep. Then, follow that with one more breath, even slower than before.
>
> -----   -----
>
> Now, visualize the following and, if you are comfortable, move with the eagle -- BE the eagle. If you are not comfortable doing the actions, use visualization, which with practice can be just as powerful.
>
> » Arms out, as if you are soaring...graceful, riding the wind for several minutes.
> » Now you are circling, wheeling, gliding... for several minutes.
> » Next, you are traveling, beating the wind and diving... for several minutes.
> » Now, again, you are soaring, gliding, circling... for several minutes.
>
> -----   -----
>
> As you see your nest, you circle and gently hover and finally settle into your nest and relax.
>
> *Continued on next page...*

EXERCISE 4.3   THE EAGLE MEDITATION (CONTINUED)

    You are one with the eagle and with God.
    Stretch and become aware of your body.
        Become aware of your state of mind.
        How are you feeling right now?

      -----   -----

Next, Take a deep breath and relax, contemplating the message you have received.

Take one more slow comfortable deep breath and as you exhale....

Bring yourself back to the awareness of the room in which you now find yourself.

      -----   -----

And when you feel ready, slowly open your eyes. If you wish, begin to slowly stretch your neck and shoulders, and then think to yourself about how great this sense of peace and quietness feels throughout your mind and body.

And with confidence, you are ready to begin a new day.

      -----   -----

We know that if we change our movements,
    we change our thoughts (because exercise releases endorphins).

The characteristics of the eagle are ours for the asking. The eagle (you)
    Sees the big picture.
    Sees opportunities.
        I am adaptable and can
        Soar above the frets of the day as I
        Ride the wind.

        ...And I can let rain roll off my back

            I am...Free....

THE SPIRIT OF LETTING GO
MINDFULNESS 101

Mindfulness is a form of meditation, a mental state in which you practice calm awareness of your thoughts, actions or motivations. By practicing mindfulness, you can observe your thoughts, actions and motivations from a place of detachment and realize that thoughts are just thoughts. These thoughts are your interpretations of the truth (ego interpretations), not who you are. By recognizing this, you are then free to release a thought (letting it go), having realized that the thought may not be concrete reality or absolute truth. This can free your mind to be more creative, quieting the left rational/logical brain and allowing the right brain to speak.

An example of this recognizing and letting go process is the day I broke my mother's car. Not easy to do just sitting in a parked car, but I did it. It was 1992, I was 35 years old, just back from Texas, and I was using my mother's car until mine arrived. I had one of those A-line winter coats that were so popular at the time, and as I went to get into the car, the pocket of the coat caught the blinker arm and snapped it off. Instant flashback: I'm 16 years old, and I have to tell my parents that I smashed the car. Flash forward: I sat there in an absolute panic -- I had just relocated from Texas and was stressed to the max. I was coping with my mother in hospice, a new job, and a sister who lovingly told a shop assistant, "Elaine is homeless." So I sat there, in my mother's broken car, and I took a few deep breaths. As my mind quieted, my mother's greatest piece of advice came in handy: "What's the worst that could happen?" I was able to practice mindfulness, evaluating and letting go of my awfulizing thoughts and feelings, realized that I was now an adult; I did have a job, however insecure and low-paying, and I would just get it fixed. But I still remember that break-into-a-cold-sweat-moment of panic -- *"I broke my mother's car!"*

As you spend time practicing this state of mindfulness, closely observe your own reality. While doing this, you start realizing that happiness starts when you can let go of your attachment to thoughts. Hanging onto toxic thoughts or issues hurts only ourselves. It is the interpretations that we put on such things as our thoughts, our past and the outcomes that drive our automatic reactions. It is our perceptions that drive our stress. The practice of mindfulness can train us to disengage the automatic pilot of our behaviors and emotions.

Mindfulness is also what we choose to turn our attention to every day. For instance, when we wake up and our mind is already on that meeting with the boss and the deadline we have to tell him we will not make, how does that color our morning? Borrowed-from-the-future reactions can make us abrupt with our spouse and kids and ready to kick the dog when he won't come when called and makes our coffee taste like sawdust. What has happened here? Have we set ourselves up for success? No. We have just reinforced our worst-case scenario. We have, indeed, created our own reality. How relaxed will we be as we go into that room? How creative will we be? Not surprisingly, research shows that people demonstrate poor creativity when under stress. We have made the natural and automatic choice of paying attention to -- being mindful of -- the worst scenario.

Let's do an instant rewind. Instead of anticipating the worst scenario, envision five minutes of mindfulness on awakening. Listen to the birds at the feeder just outside the window as we brush our teeth. Observe our 2-year-old stretch his boundaries as he lifts the juice carton and spills it…well, he lifted it 2 inches higher than last week. Observe the dog, frolicking and free and just glad to be alive. Our mind is focused on the here and now, this moment in time, just being. Making the choice to be mindful of the beauty of this moment has created for us a place of calm and peace, with appreciation for, and joy in every living thing. If we know something is going to worry us upon wakening, put a reminder to be mindful where we will see it first thing in the morning. Do not give worry a chance to wind us up.

Being in the moment

All you have is this moment. It is only in this moment that you can feel joy.

Therefore, if you need more joy in your life, you need to practice being in the moment. This is the only place you will find it

Thick Naht Hanh, a Tibetan monk, tells us in his book *True Love* that mindfulness brings us back to the present moment, helps us in this space to touch nonfear, and it is only here that you can experience total relief, total happiness. That deadline is not you. Not meeting the deadline is not you. YOU are the choices you make. Choosing true mindfulness makes you at peace as you walk into the boss's office.

> Laughter captures a moment of joy
> and emphasizes the divine in all of us

EXERCISE 4.4   BEING IN THE MOMENT

1) Start with just 15 minutes each day.
2) Just relax, wherever you are, whomever you're with.
3) Relax your shoulders, letting them drop.
4) Focus your attention on what you are doing, whom you are with.
5) If you are with someone, what is he/she saying, doing?
6) How are you reacting…how do you want to act?
7) Consciously bring your attention back if it wanders. Don't chastise yourself, just refocus.
8) Are there distractions that you can get rid of?
9) Be in wonder of the moment, your ability to be here, experiencing this, being with the person you are with: listening, smelling, seeing, tasting, touching and feeling. What is there in this for you to learn?

> **EXERCISE 4.5   CONSCIOUS HUGGING**
>
> When you hug someone, breathe in and out slowly three times and your happiness will be multiplied by at least tenfold.
>
> <u>Essential Writings</u>, Thich Nhat Hanh

> **EXERCISE 4.6   CONTINUOUS MINDFULNESS**
>
> Pick an event that happens frequently during your day that you are often and naturally aware of, such as:
>
> 1) Bells on a local church chiming the hour.
> 2) Stoplights.
> 3) Breathing.
>
> Every time this occurs, take three deep breaths, focusing on the air coming in and the air going out. If that is all you have time for, great. If you have more time, take 60 seconds and just sit there, eyes open or closed, whichever ever you prefer. Say some phrase that has meaning for you – e.g., "Every breath is prayer."

A STORY OF SURRENDER: THE POWER OF LETTING GO

I am the third of four girls, and I have never been a passive person, as the people who know me well will be happy to tell you. We had a cruel, standing joke in our family that the two older girls are "well-shut-up" and the two younger ones -- well, I'll let you fill in the blanks. We were never able to see and laugh at the following setup until much later in life. Imagine if you will, four teenaged girls sitting at the dinner table, Mom at one end and Dad at the other. We were expected to speak only when spoken to (this was the early '70s, believe it or not). Dad talked of his day – with its trials and tribulations. The rest of us tried to sit still, but then my older sister would make faces to get me in trouble. Then there was the choking in the middle of a mouthful of milk, etc. And when it came to cleaning up and doing the dishes (by hand, despite the presence of a dishwasher), can you imagine the four teenaged girls doing it quietly? Because, of course, Dad was watching the news (i.e., snoozing in front of the TV). Yah, right, like we were successful at that, too. So in retaliation to those ridiculous expectations, I am NOT one of the well-shut-up Scribner girls.

Knowing this, you can imagine how I have struggled with the seemingly passive wisdom of turn the other cheek and surrendering your will. I still struggle with it, but age has mellowed me, and I now realize that it all comes out in the end and I pick my battles. Or I waste my own time. And what does it REALLY mean in the grand scheme of things, after all?

The other day, while I was washing dishes (quietly of course), I saw a bowl on the window sill where I keep wishbones. Since my daughter is now 23, we were out of the habit of using them, so I had quite a collection. But as I was pondering those wishbones, I think at long last I truly understood the power of surrender. It is actually an energy force. When two people are holding onto the wishbone, if you simply hold it without any force at all, most of the time you will get the larger portion.

Parable of the Wishbone

If you are the one who resists
and tries to make your will dominate,

you are the one who gets the smaller part,
the one whose wish does not come true,

the one with the proverbial short end of the stick.

Elaine Scribner, 2011

Verse 17 of the Tao Te Ching tells us that surrender is also a management tool. "With the greatest leader above them, people barely know one exists....He works without self-interest and leaves no trace. When all is finished, the people say, 'We did it ourselves'" (translation by Wayne W. Dyer).

The practice of T'ai Chi Ch'uan is all about harmonizing with the universe, moving in unison with it and moving with the flow of nature. This concept is called Wu-wei, or nothing-doing.

So remember the lessons of the wishbone...the power of surrender, the power of letting go. It is the first step to success.

Chapter 5
THE POWER OF LOVE

> Love is more a conscious decision than it is an emotion.
> *Mindful Loving*, Henry Grayson

Love. Maybe it's not surprising that the country known for its stiff upper lip and un-emotionalism has only one word to describe a number of emotions from affection to romantic attachment. The Greek language, on the other hand, has four. The study of neurolinguistics demonstrates that language frames our understanding and adds depth to it. Having only one word makes for a shallow understanding of what is perhaps our most important emotion. Below are the Greek words for love and their definitions. I think the distinctions in "eros" and "philia" are particularly interesting and helpful in understanding the various directions that love can take as it matures.

Greek Words for Love

Agape	Selfless, altruistic, spiritual, unconditional love.
Philia	Friendship, loyalty to friends, family and community. Requires virtue, equality and familiarity.
Eros	Passionate love. You feel more than philia. You may initially feel passion, but with time the relationship may become platonic and an appreciation for beauty.
Storge	Affection, as for children; or acceptance of situations: loving the tyrant.

Jewish and Biblical traditions use compassion, empathy, altruism, kindness and love interchangeably. According to Christian tradition, charity is compassion in action. Hindu traditions hold compassion, along with charity and self-control, as one of three central virtues. Compassion is at the very heart of the Buddha's teachings, as that which helps to relieve suffering. The Buddha, said *"Compassion is that which makes the heart of the good move at the pain of others. It crushes and destroys the pain of others…it shelters and embraces the distressed"* (*Bhagavad-Gita*).

This section on love discusses tools to use in relationships and how we can relate to ourselves, with compassion, kindness and forgiveness.

COMPASSION

I have come to understand that most behaviors, if not of love, are fear-based. Realizing this makes it easier to be compassionate with people who are fearful and acting out of fear.

We live in a society that can easily cause us to live in a perpetual state of fear. Much of it expresses itself as mild forms of road rage or sniping at salespeople. The threats around us are many, whether from natural causes (saber-toothed tigers and traffic), or inflicted by ourselves or others. When we are not able to resolve these fears, our bodies remain in a perpetual state of fight-or-flight -- chronic stress. Media and the news emphasize the terrors and tragedies of the world while consumerism exploits our fears. In the '60s we did not want to have a ring around our husband's collar, or non-flaky pie crusts. Today we certainly do not want to be seen with an outdated telephone -- we might get the message one minute later than everyone else and, in the meantime, we chewed someone out for not inviting us to the office potluck. Heaven forbid that we should touch a door handle or exercise equipment that someone else has touched without disinfecting it first. Then there's global warming: will recycling and conversion to CFS lightbulbs be enough? Fear permeates all aspects of our life and behavior.

> If it isn't love, it is fear.

My shelves are full of books from my management era, such as that wonderfully handy *Coping with Difficult People*, *When the Going gets Rough* and *Office Warfare*, not to mention *The Leadership Secrets of Attila the Hun*. Looking at these tomes, it is clear that fear is the common denominator in people who need to defend their territory against new people, new ideas and new technology. Fear that someone will take their job; fear that someone else will take the credit; fear that someone will take their job and the credit; fear of failure; or even fear that we might succeed. And so we undermine our efforts.

Listen to the labels given "difficult people":

- Hostile-aggressives
- Sherman tanks
- Snipers
- Exploders
- The complainer (powerless or refuses responsibility)
- The silent and unresponsive person
- The super-agreeables
- Wonderfully nice people (until you need action)
- The wet blanket/negativists (deflate your optimism)
- The know-it-alls (superior, condescending or pompous, making you feel like an idiot)
- The indecisive stallers (cannot let go until it is perfect, which is never)

(*Coping with Difficult People...in business and in life.*, Bramson)

Every label speaks of fear. What you can bring to such situations is compassion, kindness, joy and freedom. At the very least, you will be happy in yourself. You may perhaps even set an example that may not affect your immediate time and space, but others may see, learn and apply after seeing your calm in the storm. Research by Nicholas Christakis, indicates that our happiness is affected by people three degrees removed from us. That's a friend of a friend of a friend. And in the meantime, *you* have remained intact, at peace, with only temporary squalls happening on your own emotional front. When I was a supervisor and nursing director, I was not one to participate in office games, and my clinics were a bastion of relative peace in the otherwise turbulent waters. Contemporary wisdom said I could not do it, that I could not create a unit of peace and quality when the rest of the organization did not buy in. Never being one to take no for an answer, I created my own island anyway. Maybe it lasted only two years, but it was the right thing to do. Fifteen years later, I can still say that.

I was watching a PBS documentary a while ago in which men who were bouncing between jail, mental institutions and homeless shelters were interviewed. What struck me forcibly was that, just as they started feeling better, feeling confident that they had licked this thing, they would stop taking their medications. They knew they were cured. Soon, however, they started decompensating (functionally deteriorating). They shared their thoughts on-screen during their decompensation. Their thoughts and imaginings were all fear-based. Whatever happened in their distant past that created these images is too horrific to think about.

Exercise the Compassion Muscle

This muscle needs exercising. Understanding comes with compassion. At work, at school, at play -- whenever there is a disagreement, look to understand, walk the proverbial mile in the other person's shoes and find a solution that fits. If you have no apparent avenues in your life to challenge you this way, volunteer. It gets you outside of yourself. Choose anything that appeals to you, but best is a service where you have direct contact with people, such as a nursing home, Big Brothers/Big Sisters, or a homeless shelter. At home, practice conscious listening (Exercise 3.7) to increase your understanding and thereby your compassion. In working with the most vulnerable, we can come to understand and accept our own frailties.

Henry Grayson, in his book *Mindful Loving,* finds the English definition of love too constricting. He says we need to redefine love because it's not so much an emotion as a "conscious, willful decision." He goes on to say that this is easy when the object(s) of our love are being what we want -- the real test comes when things get difficult, times "when we perceive rejection or attack -- times when we might ordinarily become angry or critical...When we understand the true nature of love, we realize that we can love even when we don't feel like it."

> "I feel from my own experience that when I practice compassion, there is an immediate direct benefit to myself. I get 100 percent while others might get 50 percent."
>
> The Dalai Lama

KINDNESS

Kindness is an act or a state of being. "True kindness is a strong, genuine, warm way of being. It is the result of interplay among qualities, such as warmth, trust, patience, loyalty, gratitude, and many others" (*The Power of Kindness*).

All major religions and philosophies of the world value kindness. Christianity defines love as being "patient and kind..." (I Corinthians); Catholicism takes it further, considering kindness to be one of the seven virtues; the Talmud claims that "deeds of kindness are equal in weight to all the commandments"; Mettā, one of the Ten Perfections in Buddhism, is usually translated into English as "loving kindness". The Dalai Lama states, "My religion is kindness"; and Confucius urged his followers to "recompense kindness with kindness."

Piero Ferrucci puts it succinctly, stating, "...we are going through an Ice Age of the heart [which]....goes hand in hand with the epidemic of depression and panic attacks...." The power of kindness, people need it.

Current studies find that kindness is the most desired trait in a mate. When 16,000 people from 37 cultures around the world were asked about their most desired traits in a mate, for both sexes, the first preference was kindness (D. M., Buss).

Research has also found that kind people are healthier and live longer, are more popular and productive, have greater success in business, and are happier than others (*The Power of Kindness*). A Harvard study started in the 1950s was reevaluated 35 years later (M.A. Herman, and S.M. McHale). The study looked at the effects of parental characteristics on the health of their children later in life. The results were dramatic, as the table below demonstrates.

Frequency of Health Conditions Diagnosed in Midlife

Health Conditions	Parent Characteristics: warm, patient and affectionate	Parent Characteristics: impatient, cold, and brutal.
Major disease: coronary artery disease, hypertension, duodenal ulcer and alcoholism	45% of the cohort	91% of the cohort

Exercise the Kindness Muscle

If you are uncertain where to start living joyously, I believe that the best place to start is exercising the kindness muscle. If you start with kindness, understanding and compassion will follow. Kindness is action; compassion is the understanding. If you must, fake it until you make it.

EXERCISE 5.1 ENRICH YOUR LIFE: PRACTICE RANDOM ACTS OF KINDNESS

Minimum: Once a day
What are some things you could do?

_____
_____
_____

> One of the most effective techniques for transforming your life is to
>
> "…just be a little kinder."
>
> *The Dalai Lama*

EXERCISE 5.2   EMOTIONAL TRANQUILITY MEDITATION

1) Think of all the kind things you have done and do now in your life.
2) Show kindness to someone you love.
3) Show kindness to someone you feel neutral about.
4) Show kindness to a difficult person.

(Mental Resilience)

FORGIVENESS

When you forgive, you heal yourself. Even if you do not see a change or response in the other person, you are healed. Though the lack of response or change in the other person can be frustrating, even infuriating, forgiveness is actually more about you than about them.

> "Resentment or grudges do no harm to the person against whom you hold these feelings, but every day and every night of your life, they are eating at you."
>
> *Norman Vincent Peale*

When you forgive, you heal yourself. Even if you do not see a change or response in the other person, you are healed. Though the lack of response or change in the other person can be frustrating, even infuriating, forgiveness is actually more about you than about them.

> To err is human…to forgive, divine
> *Alexander Pope*

What is Forgiveness?

According to Simon and Simon in their book on forgiveness, forgiveness is often the missing "peace" you are seeking, whether it is forgiving yourself or others for the disappointments, the "not good enough" messages, the abandonment, the ridicule, the deceptions and abuse that gave us pain and shattered our sense of trust.

What would forgiveness look like? To me, it would be peaceful and calm, like waves gently lapping the shore or the wind rustling the leaves of my walnut trees -- my sanctuary at its best. Non-forgiveness is angst and anger and feels like chaos and pain.

I would respectfully suggest that most if not all unresolved issues involve the lack of forgiveness. Forgiveness is a choice we have every minute of every day, even for such minor infractions as the driver who cut you off in traffic, your boss who embarrassed you in a meeting, or your significant other for making a work commitment on your anniversary. It is important to know that forgiveness is a decision, not an emotion, and that it is possible to forgive (one person's choice) without reconciling (two people who reestablish mutual trust). Forgiveness is a choice, and when faced with a situation where you have been hurt, you have two choices. You can either forgive the person, or you can hold onto bitterness and anger. There is no room for both. The presence of bitterness and anger or coldness and distance, even if it is righteous anger, is a sign that you have not truly forgiven.

Forgiveness is also one of the many faces of kindness. It is kindness at work. When we forgive, compassion reasserts itself, we let go of the negative thoughts and feelings that have become part of the situation, we give up being stuck and allow our own healing, setting our time and energy free. Forgiveness is truly a gift that we give ourselves.

Not surprisingly, forgiveness research has found that people who will not forgive tend to have more negative health indicators: more stress-related disorders, lower immune system function, and higher rates of cardiovascular disease (Everett Worthington, Jr.).

> "Anger is like a hot stone. If you pick it up to throw at someone, you will get burned."
> *Ancient proverb*

Exercise the Forgiveness Muscle

At some point the bitterness, anger and angst will grow old. Trying something new will have its appeal, even if it is work. And it will be work. Completing unfinished business will be both time-consuming and possibly painful. But peace and freedom are the rewards. "Forgiveness is accepting that nothing we do to punish *them* will heal *us*" (Simon and Simon).

Ask Yourself

Is protecting yourself from possible pain worth missing out on peace and freedom?

In their book *Forgiveness: How to Make Peace with Your Past and Get On With Your Life,* husband and wife team Simon and Simon spell out six stages of forgiveness and resolution.

1. Denial.
2. Self-blame.
3. Victimization (the woe-is-me/misery-loves-company party).
4. Indignation/anger.
5. Survivor state – reassessing/reasserting your self-worth.
6. Integration stage – forgiving and getting on with your life (vs. moving through the paces and putting in time). Acceptance, according to Brian Luke Seaward, "…is perhaps the most important muscle of the soul to exercise, particularly with things we have absolutely no control over." [This is what I call the thrivivor state (a thriving survivor).]

All of these stages are normal and natural -- it is getting stuck in any one of them that becomes unhealthy. For instance, holding a grudge, and staying angry is to get stuck in stage four of forgiveness resolution and is as futile as it is self-defeating. Self-victimization results in a sour view of life, such as "Life is tough and then you die," or being perpetually on guard and defensive.

When we become stuck in anger, resentful and defensive, we are allowing someone else or a situation to control us and our emotions. We are allowing ourselves to be victimized. Consider my friend Nancy's situation. At a very young age she was a victim of repeated sexual abuse from a teenaged uncle in her own home. Fifty-five years later, in her late 50s, she still suffers from chronic debilitating migraines. Whenever I speak with her, her fuzzy voice tells me she is either on medication for a bout of migraines or is in what I call the postmigraine syndrome (sluggishness, fuzzy brain, slowed thinking). A couple of years ago her father died. She and her father still had not resolved the belief/disbelief issues surrounding the abuse. Though he was compassionate for her pain, this was his brother they were talking about. During his illness and the months after his death, Nancy's family trod warily around her, never sure when or what would set off another round of anger, recriminations and paranoia. That these were directly related to the abuse, there can be no doubt. She herself verified this by telling one sister, "I know you've always thought I was a slut," and another family member "If we allow Phil into the state to visit Dad, no one will be safe, he'll find you" (despite marriage, name changes, etc.).

Nancy's whole life is affected by this anger and bitterness. She is physically and emotionally in pain while Phil goes his merry way (the statue of limitations having long ago run out). She has not yet found her way to complete the forgiveness cycle to come to resolution. She is continuing to allow herself to be victimized. There is no doubt she was a victim. She was an innocent child to whom horrific things were done. Fifty-five years later, she is continuing to allow herself to be victimized by the situation and the lack of justice instead of being happy and whole, to the great sadness of her friends and family. Such a waste.

There are many signs that can tell us that we may still have issues with anger, such as depression, drinking and desire for revenge. Katherine Piderman contends that the following signs may also indicate that we are still held hostage by our anger: dwelling on the event (mud mind, mind rut), having a chip on our shoulder, self-pity, emotional outbursts, being avoided, feelings of being misunderstood, feeling at odds with your values or beliefs. Other behaviors that may provide clues that we are holding onto anger are avoiding people and being cold or distant.

"The emotional distress of long-held hurts causes exhaustion. It can contribute to feelings of depression, agitation, and anger. It is like a virus on your hard drive (the subconscious mind), which every now and then causes your computer to break down" (*Mental Resilience*).

EXERCISE 5.3   NINE STEPS TOWARD FORGIVENESS

Journaling through each of the following steps can be an extremely helpful and healing process in your progress toward resolving forgiveness issues.

1. Acknowledge your emotions. Whether you are angry, hurt, ashamed or embarrassed (or some combination of the above), acknowledge your emotional reaction to the wrongdoing.

2. Go beyond identifying the person who hurt you and articulate the specific behaviors that upset or hurt you.

3. Make the choice to forgive.

4. Explain to yourself why you made the decision to forgive. Your reasons can be as practical as wanting to be free of the anger so that you can concentrate better at work.

5. Attempt to "walk in the shoes" of the other person. Consider that person's vulnerabilities.

6. Make a commitment not to pass along the pain you have endured—even to the person who hurt you in the first place.

Continued on next page...

> **EXERCISE 5.3   NINE STEPS TOWARD FORGIVENESS**
> **(CONTINUED)**
>
> 7. Decide instead to offer the world mercy and good will. At this stage, you may wish to reconcile with the other person (but that is not necessary).
>
> 8. Reflect on how it feels to let go of a grudge. Find meaning in the suffering you experienced and overcame.
>
> 9. Discover the paradox of forgiveness: as you give the gift of forgiveness to others, you receive the gift of peace.
>
> *Adapted from Robert Enright*

Forgiving Yourself: To Err is Human

Mistakes happen. Trial and error is how we learn many of our lessons. We have to be willing to forgive ourselves. Holding onto anger, frustration and disgust with yourself can be just as toxic as holding onto resentment against someone else. Be compassionate. Recognize that poor behavior or mistakes do not make you worthless or bad. Identify changes you might need to make to avoid similar mistakes in the future. Let go and move on.

> ## *Presence*
>
> *All you have is this moment... not the past, not the future. How do you want to spend it?*
>
> Unease, anxiety, tension, stress, worry — all forms of fear — are caused by too much future and not enough presence. Guilt, regret, resentment, grievances, sadness, bitterness, and all forms of nonforgiveness are caused by too much past and not enough presence.
>
> *Eckhart Tolle*

A Story of Amish Grace
October 2, 2006

I stand in awe of the members of the Amish community at West Nickle Mines School in Pennsylvania. On October 2, 2006, they extended comfort and forgiveness to the family of the man responsible for the shooting of ten young girls, five of whom died. The seemingly unforgivable was forgiven.

"Letting go of grudges" is a deeply rooted value in Amish culture. The Amish [people's] willingness to forgo vengeance does not undo the tragedy or pardon the wrong, but rather constitutes a first step toward a future that is more hopeful.

It is clear to me, here on the outside of this tragedy, that forgiveness is the only way to healing. I can only hope that I could be so strong, so wise, if I was in a similar situation.

EXERCISE 5.4   GIVE IT SOME THOUGHT

Do you have some unforgiven people or issues in your closet? Resentments that you are harboring?

_____

_____

_____

Revisit Exercise 5.3 and journal through the issues you identified.

THE POWER OF SAYING I'M SORRY

"Love means never having to say I'm sorry." Hogwash. We all put our feet in our mouths from time to time, and our loved ones may not always be able to sort it out. Pride gets in the way and stubbornness sets in: "I'm not going to give in, I'm right, you're wrong." But there can be no pride in the real practice of love. Instead it is the ego that steps in, under the aegis of protecting the self, and will not allow you to say I'm sorry.

> "We deserve to be at peace with ourselves and others."
> *Melody Beattie*

So many feelings are associated with saying "I'm sorry," making us fearful and defensive: fear of blame, shame, liability; exchange of power, vulnerability, humiliation. I grew up in a grudge-holding family culture, which often resulted in the silent treatment. This practice is a self-perpetuating monster, making it harder as time goes on to break through and reestablish relationships. If we could only change the paradigm from seeing the words "I'm sorry" as a sign of weakness to seeing them as a sign of wisdom and healing, seeing them as a part of our learning curve as sentient beings. I would elaborate on this, that it is even greater to say "I'm sorry" and forgive than to be forgiven. It is important to recognize that saying "I'm sorry" can be overused, a quick fix for ongoing bad behavior. If that is happening, personal reflection and concrete change may be called for. Additionally, making amends may also be needed.

The ABC's of making an apology/of making amends

- » Sincerity, attitude, honesty, openness and willingness to forgive; trusting your timing and intuition are important facets of making an apology.
- » Keep in mind an attitude of win – win: the process itself must not be self-defeating or hurtful – that only perpetuates a grudge-holding mode.

- Express regret — I'm so sorry that….
- Acknowledge the injury — I caused you pain (distress).
- Make amends — Is there anything I can do to make this better?

» Asking for forgiveness is not appropriate. It is something that needs to be offered by the other party.

» Explanations: Not excuses, but sometimes an explanation, an analysis of how it happened, is useful because it fosters understanding and real change. Many times people do not want to hear this, and regardless of how it is meant, these explanations are taken as excuses. There is no crystal ball to tell us when explanations will be accepted/not accepted. But a rule of thumb is that when an adversarial role or built-in animosity in a role exists, explanations are less likely to be understood. An example of this would be supervisor to employee because of the power structure. Issues between family members may be another case where the simple, sincere, heartfelt "I'm sorry for the pain I caused you" is the best that you can do.

Even when you are in the right, "I'm sorry" is still the best win-win approach. You can express it in the following way:

» I am sorry that this disagreement has come between us.

» I'm sorry that this has come between us, that it has caused you distress. I miss our friendship.

» I'm sorry this has caused a rift. I wouldn't hurt you for anything. Can we agree to disagree?

A Tragic Accident

Even our institutions have been designed to be fearful of saying I'm sorry. Below are two examples of the institutional monster we have created.

Healthcare workers wanting to express regrets for the

loss of a loved one are in many instances prevented from doing so because of liability issues. There is legislation being proposed to protect healthcare providers while allowing them to offer comfort.

- - -   - - -

A poignant example of this is when a friend of mine was driving due-west into the sunset a number of years ago. There were children playing off to her right, near the road, that she was keeping a watchful eye on. A bicyclist veered into the path of her car. The bicyclist was dead at the scene. My friend was so cut up that her voice was totally unrecognizable to her spouse. A lifetime of regret.

My friends' insurance company had instructed the couple to have no communication with the family, not even the words of sympathy that they so wanted to express. They were threatened with having their coverage dropped if they did so.

The case was thrown out of criminal court, but the bicyclist's family pursued the case in civil court, to no avail. My friends heard through the grapevine that the family did this because they felt there was no remorse, that no expression of sympathy had been extended.

A product of our litigious society...our institutions are dehumanizing us.

Consider being the first to say I'm sorry...*EVEN IF YOU'RE RIGHT!* **You can be sorry for the misunderstanding and the pain that it caused.**

Justice and Retribution or Amnesty and Forgiveness
A Story of Tribal Grace and Dignity

Desmond Tutu in his book *No Future Without Forgiveness* describes the process by which he guided South Africa through the painful healing of a nation when apartheid ended. Reconciliation took place by having individuals come forward and acknowledge the past (stating the specifics of their crimes). The individuals gave face and identity to the anonymous, the marginalized people who had been abused for so long and were granted amnesty in exchange for full disclosure.

South Africa established the Truth and Reconciliation Commission, which looked at and rejected the two extreme methods of handling such crimes (Nuremberg trials and blanket amnesty). Commission members instead opted for a third way, which was in keeping with a feature of the African way called "ubuntu" in the Nguni group of languages. Ubuntu is a concept that holds that "my humanity is caught up, is inextricably bound up in yours" or "a person is a person through other persons" and is therefore diminished when others are treated poorly. What dehumanizes you inexorably dehumanizes me.

They would not give further life to the crimes against them but chose a way of grace and dignity.

Chapter 6
BALANCE

> **Practice Timely Procrastination.**

High levels of stress can lead to stress exhaustion symptoms (see Chapter 12). These symptoms can affect all facets of our lives: physical, mental, emotional, social and functional. Stress takes a long-term toll on brain health, even if the only damage that ensues from it is an increase in blood pressure. It is possible to manage stress, and stress management gets more efficient the more you practice. Though we cannot eliminate stress completely, we can learn to prevent much of it and manage the rest of it effectively. Some of the main principles are those that we have already discussed: care for ourselves, love ourselves and manage our *health* care.

Taoism speaks eloquently on the subject of balance. Balance encompasses patience, harmony and timing of life events. Timing of life events means to move with the flow rather than against events. Years before I had ever read Taoist philosophy I had coined the phrase "timely procrastination." When I had a problem to solve or even someone to call and I could not figure out how to do so gracefully, or the answers I was coming up with just did not fit, I would procrastinate until it felt right. More often than not, the answer was in itself timely and apropos. Timely procrastination.

Another favorite phrase that helps keep me balanced is "everything in moderation." Practicing balance in all aspects of our lives promotes and maintains inner peace. In this chapter, we will explore many of the structural items in our lives that need our care and attention. We will explore everything from sleep and time management to exercise and laughter. We will discuss stress and strategies to decrease our stress load. Stress is inevitable, but it can be managed. Managing stress is all about making choices that promote balance.

"THE ENOUGHNESS PRINCIPLE"

"Enoughness" says there is enough love, happiness, beauty and even material things for everyone…including you.

My ego struggles with this periodically… that little voice in my head that says,

> **Everything in moderation**

"What about that last Cabbage Patch doll…there weren't enough," or "My spouse didn't love me enough to stay and work this out." This is the ego proclaiming, "I am a victim." Each time I have to choose: "will I accept that," or will I step back and consider the grand scheme of things? Someone else's love for me, is, in fact, a secondhand emotion. The real question is: "Is there enough love inside of me to meet the world?" And what about that Cabbage Patch doll? There weren't enough in the store that fateful Christmas. Though my child's heart may have been set on it, there are many other dolls in the world that need adopting. Every doll is precious. Every doll needs love and a home. (You could have a lot of fun with the life lessons in this analogy.)

The term "abundance" is frequently bandied about, as well as "Don't sweat the small stuff…make the stuff bigger." Many are quoting the parable of the loaves and fishes from the New Testament as proof of the value of abundance. I prefer the humbler philosophy of enoughness. There was enough food for everyone to have their fill; the little that was left over is proof of that. It was abundance of the heart. A miracle of agape and philia, two of the four Greek words for love. Love was the true miracle. And everyone had enough.

SIMPLICITY

> "To the sage
> All of life is a movement toward perfection,
> So what need has he
> For the excessive, the extravagant, or the extreme?"
>
> *Tao te Ching*

Simple living, also known as minimalism, is a movement as ancient as Lao Tzu, the Buddha and Jesus Christ. It was embraced by St. Francis of Assisi, Henry David Thoreau and Ghandi. It is characterized by minimizing the "more is better" pursuit of wealth and consumption. People choose it for a variety of reasons, from spirituality and stress reduction to ecological and frugality convictions. Strict minimalism may not be for all of us, but many areas of our lives could benefit from decluttering.

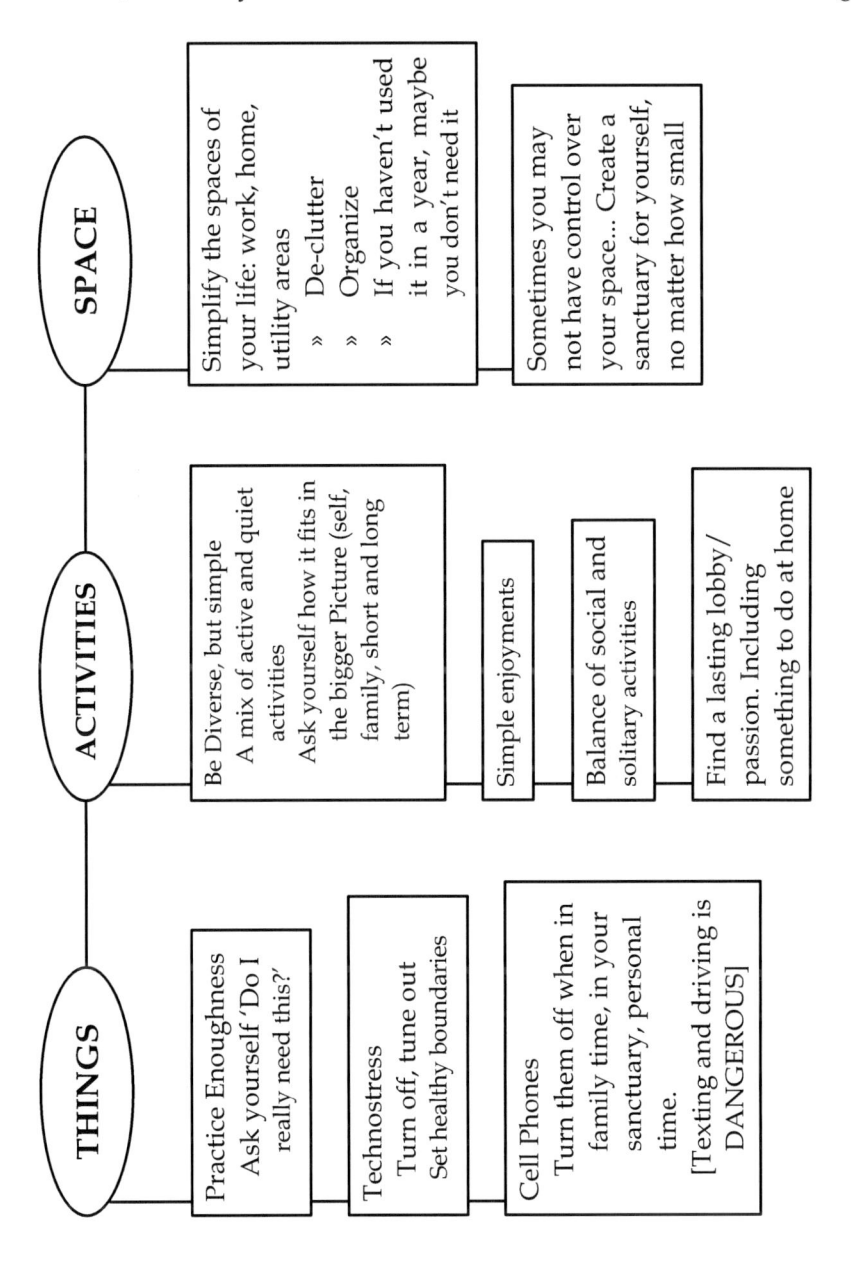

SPACE

- Simplify the spaces of your life: work, home, utility areas
  » De-clutter
  » Organize
  » If you haven't used it in a year, maybe you don't need it
- Sometimes you may not have control over your space... Create a sanctuary for yourself, no matter how small

ACTIVITIES

- Be Diverse, but simple
- A mix of active and quiet activities
- Ask yourself how it fits in the bigger Picture (self, family, short and long term)
- Simple enjoyments
- Balance of social and solitary activities
- Find a lasting lobby/passion. Including something to do at home

THINGS

- Practice Enoughness
- Ask yourself 'Do I really need this?'
- Technostress
- Turn off, tune out
- Set healthy boundaries
- Cell Phones
- Turn them off when in family time, in your sanctuary, personal time.
- [Texting and driving is DANGEROUS]

Ten things you'll want to do
1. Spend time each day in nature.
2. Learn to enjoy silence.
3. Slow down.
4. Figure out what you *do not* want in your life.
5. Release your attachment to possessions.
6. Just say no.
7. Get your finances under control.
8. Develop gratitude.
9. Take time to think.
10. Stop the world—you can get off.

Shopping and storage spaces
1. Make a list.
2. Stick to it.
3. Groceries: Consider having the makings for two or three of each meal. I always have extra canned tomatoes. Rationale: one to cook and one spare in case of a crowd or if I cannot get to the grocery store before I make it again.
4. Closets: Unless there's a specific need to keep it, if it hasn't been used in a year, get rid of it (exceptions might be yarn, evening dress, etc., though it must still fit the space and the door must be able to close).
5. See also "Money Matters."

Three points about your peace of mind
1. Reduce your need to be in-the-know.
2. We have survived millions of years without cell phones, without being perpetually on-call. Be selective about turning yours on.
3. Consider keeping a land line and give out your cell phone number for emergency and close friends and family only.

Fifteen points about the real stuff: spirituality/simplicity
1. Learn to listen to your inner voice.
2. Learn to enjoy solitude.
3. Learn to do nothing.
4. Do a retreat.
5. Check your breathing.
6. Explore meditation.
7. Create joy in your life.
8. Love a lot.
9. Rethink the beliefs of your childhood.
10. Practice detaching yourself from outcomes and things.
11. Realize the importance of self-discipline.
12. Keep your own counsel.
13. Learn to forgive.
14. Take responsibility for your life.
15. Review your day.

Adapted from: *Inner Simplicity: 100 Ways To Regain Peace and Nourish Your Soul*, Elaine St. James

Learning to slow down and simplify can be uncomfortable until we get used to it. My schedule frequently speeds up and slows down, and there is always an adjustment period when it eases up. At that point, I have this uncomfortable, nagging feeling that I should be doing something. And that something is wrong if I am not busy. I have to reassure myself that this will pass…that I do not want to rush in and fill the void but allow myself to be empty. My current adjustment is coping with an empty nest. I have the opportunity to host foreign exchange students and I am thinking long and carefully about what type of life I want. I do not want to just fill a void to just pass time. The decision needs to be for love and growth.

SLEEP

Why sleep? Even if most of us resign ourselves to this necessity – eight hours? Yes, eight hours. But there are simply too many things to do and places to go, you say. Resign yourself. Do what it takes to do the job well. Sleep affects all aspects of our waking lives: alertness, energy, mood, body weight, perception, memory, thinking, reaction time, productivity, performance, communication skills, creativity, safety and good health. Without a doubt, the better our sleep, the better our life. We will remember things faster and be able to perform tasks faster and with fewer mistakes, thereby saving all the time the extra sleep took up.

We get 90 minutes less sleep than people who lived 100 years ago. We need to learn to value sleep again and put it high on our priority list. When my daughter entered high school in the ninth grade, she felt she had earned the right to stay up late. After a couple of months she identified that she needed more sleep and went back to her previous sleep routine. No pun intended, but the difference was night and day. What I had thought was normal adjustment to high school (cranky, rebellious, cranky, irritable, cranky) was actually lack of sleep. I had my charming, playful daughter again, and we have never looked back…except when she is tired or hungry.

It is believed that sleep allows neurons to shut down and repair themselves. With sleep deprivation, the polluted byproducts of cell activities build up, causing problems in all aspects of our lives. During sleep the growth hormone is released, which in children promotes growth and in adults promotes the repair of tissues. During sleep, nerve signaling patterns are repeated, helping to encode memory and improve learning. It is also known that during sleep, activity decreases in the parts of the brain that control emotions, decision making and social interaction, hence allowing healing and helping to maintain optimal emotional and social functioning when we're awake.

(For further reading, *Power Sleep* by Dr. James B. Maas includes a section on sleep diagnostic tests and a peak performance sleep log, tips for exhausted parents of newborns, exasperated parents of adolescents and those caring for elderly parents, as well as a discussion of pillows and mattresses and when to call the sleep doctor.

ZzZZz_{zzzzz} Strategies

- Learn to value sleep.
- Keep a regular sleep-wake cycle, even on your day off. If you are getting less than eight hours/night, slowly increase your hours of sleep. Start by going to bed 10 minutes earlier each night.
- Have a bedtime routine that relaxes and winds you down. Slow down in those hours before sleep, allow yourself to unwind and reduce stress as much as possible.
- Sleep in a dark, quiet room that is slightly cool.
- Maintain a relaxing atmosphere in the bedroom (do not do work in bed, no TV in bedroom, uncluttered, make room dark, etc.).
- Use bed only for sleeping, that other fun thing and maybe reading.
- Take a warm bath before bed.
- Have pleasurable sexual activity.
- Consider other bedtime issues, such as a restless bed partner, including pets.
- Try some bedtime relaxation techniques and clear your mind at bedtime.
- Do not go to bed until you're sleepy. If you can not fall asleep within 20 minutes, get up and do a quiet activity and come back to bed when you are sleepy.
- Avoid trying too hard to get to sleep.
- Try a sleep mask, especially if you are a day sleeper or shift worker.
- Keep mentally stimulated during the day.
- Exercise to stay fit. Vigorous exercise needs to be done four to six hours before bedtime, to give your body time to cool down to the core body temperature that is ideal for sleeping.
- Eat a balanced diet.

- Avoid large meals or even mild exercise within two hours of bedtime.
- Avoid caffeine, alcohol and nicotine within four to six hours of bedtime. Stop smoking.
- Naps: listen to your body -- to make up sleep or if you are drowsy, take a nap. Before 3 p.m. so it doesn't interfere with falling asleep later.
- Correcting back pain: sleep with a pillow between your knees (on side) or under knees (on back), and hug a pillow. These pillows put your hips and your shoulders in good body alignment and ease back pain. It's also heavenly.
- Sleep diary: if you have trouble, note times, food, drink, bathroom visits, pain, dreams, stress levels, exercise, etc. Over time a pattern may evolve that you and/or your physician may be able to sort out (National Sleep Foundation).
- Try herbs or lowest dose melatonin and give them time to work. Stop them immediately if they seem to disagree with you at all.
- Read directions and warnings on any supplement. Begin at lowest dose.
- If necessary, consult a sleep specialist.

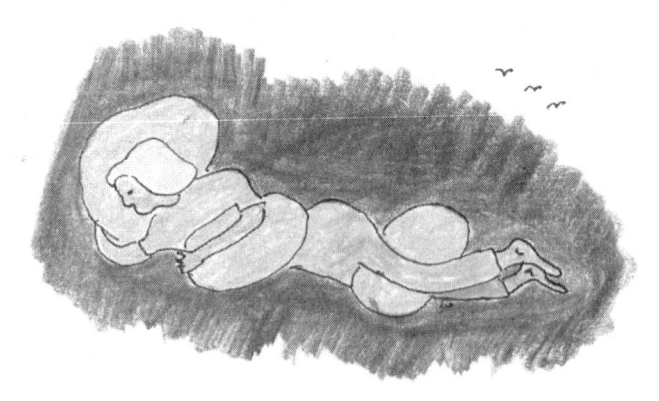

Adapted from *Getting A Good Night's Sleep*, by Muriel MacFarlane, and *Power Sleep* by Dr. James B. Maas.

TIME MANAGEMENT

Effective time management is the ability to coordinate various personal activities and responsibilities in a satisfying manner. Neurophysiologists have observed that the right hemisphere of the brain has no time perception, but its imagination and special capabilities are crucial for effective time management. This reinforces my concept of the fine art of doing nothing. I am not procrastinating, I am waiting until its time has come. Whenever possible, make a decision and move on. A balance of work and play not only provides engagement of the right brain -- also necessary for time management -- but also reinforces the need to schedule personal time. Simplify by getting rid of the technology that is eating away at your time, including TV time and texting. Keep your workspace clean, get a good night's sleep, and minimize or eliminate that 21st century affliction: multitasking. Focused attention yields results that are more effective, more timely and of better quality. Setting personal boundaries is also extremely important. Honor them.

> **Timely procrastination**

It is easy to say, "Get your priorities straight and it will all fall into place," but life *is* busy. Family demands and other commitments often happen simultaneously. Some people can naturally organize; some cannot. Simplifying helps. Prioritizing helps. But if your life is still too busy, a time management class might be in order. I do a lot of reading and a lot of planning. Two additional classes that I took that were helpful were a speed reading class and a Franklin Planner class. Doing the Yah-But Exercise (3.1) can also help. Use your journal for these exercises to help keep track of where you've been and where you want to go.

The table below is useful for managing your time. I used this table years ago for about a year and it became automatic. I now write lists this way. Its premise is that everything is ether important or not important. Then you determine if is urgent or not urgent. Be sure to include exercise, sleep and play.

EXERCISE 6.1   TIME MANAGEMENT GRID

	Urgent	Not Urgent
Important	Ex.: Clean gutters, rake leaves (snow forecasted for this weekend)	Ex: Clean refrigerator
Not Important	Ex: Interruptions, distractions	Ex: Clean up e-mail inbox, dust

WORK

I have only one thing to say about work as it relates to balance. No one on his/her death bed ever said, "I wish I'd spent more time at work." Do what you need to do at work. Give work your full attention and commitment to it while you are there. Do your best to leave work at work.

Not all of us are lucky enough to have work that is inherently satisfying. Some people must stay because of the benefits and personal circumstances. If either of these is the case, evaluate "stuckness" and burnout, and if you must stay, choose to adapt. The very act of making a conscious decision can often make all the difference. After all, the only thing in the world you can really change is your attitude.

Also see the book *PWLOARYK,* which I feel melds well with the new business concepts outlined in the *The Experience Economy*. Other great resources are *Energize your Meetings with Laughter* by Sheila Feigelson; and Kenneth Blanchard and Steven Covey's books.

MONEY MATTERS

Money management is probably one of people's top stressors.

"There never seems to be enough." Some simple tips follow. If you are in serious debt, consult your bank to ask about a safe, reliable consultant who can help consolidate your debt and teach you serious money management skills. Also, everyone can benefit by checking out Suze Orman's website, suzeorman.com. She has a lot of good, sound advice.

(1) The first principle is always to pay yourself first. If at all possible, put 10% into a retirement account with every paycheck and 5 percent into a savings account. Do it by automatic deposit and you will not even miss it.

(2) Make a budget and follow it. Carry a notebook and write down everything you spend your money on. Enter your checkbook into a spread sheet, sort it and see where your money is going. You may need to do this for only a month or so until you get a feel for where your money is going. I have done this several times throughout my life, when life and income changes occurred.

(3) Pay all of your bills on time and reserve credit cards for emergencies (medical, car, large appliance necessities). If you have to use the "buy now but pay later" option, you do not have the money.

(4) Before you buy: clean your house and use what you have, make a list before you go shopping and stick with it, don't go to the grocery store when you are hungry, do not buy on impulse, and always look for bargains.

(5) Create a sustainable lifestyle. (Be sure to read the sections on enoughness and simplifying your life.)

(6) About 15 years from retirement, get some serious financial advice and determine when/if you need to increase your investments/savings.

EXERCISE

Exercise your body -- do something you enjoy, something you can sustain. Start small. Build it up as you can. Have your partner and children do it with you. Our bodies need a mix of cardiac (aerobic) exercise, and strength and flexibility training. Start slowly and build up gradually. Do what is FUN. You may need to consult a doctor first, before starting any new form of exercise.

What follows are the best recommendations by the American College of Sports Medicine. Take all of this with a grain of salt. You must start where you are and you can only do the best you can. If you cannot make these ideals, work up to 10-minute "spurts" as tolerated. You are doing something and on the road to being the healthiest you can be. Not all of us were cut out to be Olympic champions. We can only do the best we can with what we've been given. . .

> A. At least 30 minutes of aerobic exercise at least three times a week: leisurely or brisk walking, dancing, tennis, swimming, etc. You need to get your heart rate into the cardiac zone (Google "target heart rate"). At the time this book was published, Mayo Clinic's website had clear and concise information about this.
>
> B. Additionally, strength or resistance training for each muscle group, three times each week is recommended. The muscle groups are: chest, shoulders, arms, back, abdomen, and legs. One to two exercises per muscle group is normally adequate. An average of two sets of 10 to15 repetitions of each exercise with a 2- to 3- minute rest period between sets and exercises to avoid excess fatigue.
>
> It's worth it to take a fitness class at a community college (working with a personal trainer) to learn the machines and find out more about the muscle groups.
>
> It's important to know that some exercises/machines are exercising more than one muscle group at a time.
>
> C. And flexibility exercise for balance, agility and coordination, such as yoga, tai chi, Pilates, etc. is recommended at least two times per week.

Most importantly: vary your activities to keep it interesting and fun. When time is tight, remember the 10-minute spurts, which can inch you toward your goals, decrease stress and increase your mental functioning.

Make the commitment and do it. Exercise increases cerebral blood flow, increases your mental abilities and has been shown to protect against dementia, heart disease and stroke. You work at it, and it will help you have an aging process as free of disease as you can make it. Have you watched the reality program "The Biggest Loser"? My daughter was addicted to watching it in 2008/9, so by default, I ended up watching it also. Many people came off all their heart, blood pressure and diabetic medicines from diet and exercise alone (under close supervision of a physician, of course). There is a big lesson here for all of us. It is not just the high cost of prescriptions but a drug-free, side-effect-free lifestyle. Wow. Do not try this one on your own, though. Have your physician on board with you.

A great added benefit is that engaging our large muscles (the muscles of the arms and legs) releases endorphins. Endorphins are a natural antidepressant and pain reliever. So powerful is this effect that some psychologists are beginning to require that clients start on an exercise program for two weeks before they will even consider putting them on antidepressants.

Aerobics is a great way to cover all bases with your physical exercise routine. It works on all aspects of fitness: flexibility, muscular strength, and cardiovascular fitness, often set to music. Therefore, the recommendation would be 60 minutes, at least five times each week. That might be a bit much, but adding it to the mix can add fun and a new dimension to your routine.

Water aerobics is also multi-everything. Not only is it easier on your joints, it also allows for greater range of motion than traditional aerobic exercises. It can also qualify as your resistance training. Take a couple of classes from different people, find out what activities you like to do, then make your own routine and set it to some wild and crazy music to keep you going.

I am finding that tai chi may well be the perfect exercise. It is known as meditation in motion and focuses on balanced, slow, controlled movement. Because of this, research is demonstrating its effectiveness as an adjunct therapy for many health conditions. No health problems? Physically fit? Tai chi is still for you. We are finding that people who practice tai chi one or two times per week experience less stress, decreased anxiety, better sleep, improved mood, and increased strength and energy levels.

A recent publication of the Harvard Medical School, discusses that tai chi has been found in numerous studies -- by Harvard, Stanford, Tufts University and Beth Israel in Boston, among others -- to be an effective adjunct therapy, improving function and quality of life. Further, that this low-impact exercise can be easily adapted to anyone's ability, whether physically fit, dependant on a wheelchair or even recovering from surgery. Additional research was done by the North Carolina School of Medicine and UCLA. Tai chi has been found to significantly improve depression, anxiety, energy levels, quality of life and sleep, and reduce pain. The slow and controlled exercise improves upper and lower body strength, balance and flexibility, thereby reducing falls.

I know I am beginning to sound like a snake oil salesman, but studies of people with arthritis, Parkinson's, breast cancer, stroke and heart disease, who practice tai chi, have demonstrated increased functional capacity and quality of life. Increased bone density, and lowered blood pressure, cholesterol and triglyceride levels are also among its merits. Additionally, people are experiencing decreased pain, making it ideal for those with arthritis and fibromyalgia. People experiencing dizziness and balance problems (vestibular disorders) are also benefiting from improved symptoms. This mom says, if the snake oil works -- buy it!

So, following my own advice for variety and fun, my routine looks like this:
- 10-15 minutes of yoga for flexibility every morning
- Tai chi 2 to 3 times per week
- Dance ~1 time per week (alternating contradancing, Latin/ and swing dancing)
- Bicycling 1 to 4 times per week when I can fit it in (stationary bike in the basement 1 to 2 times per week when I can't)
- [Plus the gym 1 to 2 times per week when I'm not getting enough of the other types of exercise]

It may be prosaic to say, but children take a lot of time and energy. If you are planning to have children, try to establish your exercise habits early, even before they arrive. Be sure to cultivate some family-friendly exercise: hiking, biking, swimming, Frisbee golf, cross-country skiing, tai chi, yoga, etc. The more you can include the children in what you are doing, the more you will be able to maintain your exercise schedule and build healthy habits that will be second nature to the children. As you get older, making sure you have low-impact options such as yoga, tai chi, water aerobics, will help fight the "use it or lose it" principle.

NUTRITION...Changing Habits

Eat, drink and be healthy. Yeah, yeah, you've heard it all before. But it's true. Whole grains, plant fats, fruits, vegetables and nuts, all in moderation. A diet providing 1,600 to 1,700 calories/day or less has been shown to be the best for your body and brain functioning.

Yes, it can be done. In fall 2007, having just turned 50 and seeing that next milestone hovering in the distance...the big 6-0 -- I quit Oreos. Cold turkey. I kid you not. I had had six of those crunchy, delectable morsels dunked in milk every night since elementary school. Five was too few, seven too many. I had it timed to perfection -- the amount of time needed to soak up the optimal amount of milk. "Optimal amount of milk" defined as the amount of milk it took to optimize texture and chocolate enhancement without the cookie breaking off into the milk. Then, to experience it dissolving in your mouth, with that explosion of flavor, chocolate and the creamy filling was Nirvana. Oreos and milk – a match made in heaven.

YUP, YUP, YUP. Cold turkey. I kid you not. Heartless. I just will not talk about the number of years and the number of students I had to confess my addiction to before I finally did it. For years I taught about the food pyramid and the importance of a balanced diet to my future nurse aides. Together we discovered that the food pyramid was *wrong*. At the base below the grains (pre-2007 pyramid) was chocolate, and more importantly, Oreos. And then I would confess. One of my students even drew a cartoon for me...a path of Oreos, leading to my classroom door.

Lesson: If you talk about it long enough, you will be able to do it. We are talking about lifelong changes, so keep trying.

Several years before, I started having borderline elevated

cholesterol levels. My doctor told me to go on a low cholesterol diet. Thinking that 20 years had gone by since my nursing school days and SURELY they had a simplified system by now, I asked for a copy of one. I was mailed a 1-inch stack of 8 ½- by 11- inch closely typed pages. You've got to be kidding. I'm a busy career woman. How am I going to assimilate this? And if I was intimidated by this with my training, what must the rest of the world be thinking? Anyway, I recycled that document and sat down at my computer. (I think I was weaned on spreadsheets. I think in spreadsheets.) I set up a file and pulled all the canned and frozen goods off my shelves and entered the nutrition information into the computer. Then I set up formulas to calculate how much of this and that I ate at one serving. What fun. You can now do the same thing by going to mypyramid.gov…much easier.

I discovered three areas where I could improve and make a huge difference: cheese, milk and, surprise, surprise, Oreos. So I switched from 2 percent milk to skim milk and switched to low-fat Oreos (that lasted exactly one week). I gradually decreased the amount of cheese. Not by design, but apparently by just knowing I needed to, I began making better choices. The switch to skim milk wasn't easy. It took three months of mixing the two milks until I could no longer tell the difference. But I figured it was a habit for life and a few more months wasn't going to make a big difference. The milk and cheese alone, were able to make a 10 point difference in my cholesterol and get me back in the safe zone. Of course I started looking at labels and doing all the routine stuff such as decreasing consumption of chips and bacon and taking the skin off chicken, but I had never done those to excess anyway. It all added up.

Lesson: When you have the luxury of time, take it. Take your time about making lifelong habit changes. Work them into your lifestyle. Make one easy change and make a plan for easing into a more difficult one. It's worth it. You're worth it.

Zonya Foco, is a Registered Dietician who believes that diets don't work and there is power in one good habit. So she has defined eight such habits to choose from in her program called "DIET FREE." These are wonderfully commonsense changes that you can start by picking one that works for you and really work it. Here is a summary, but if you need further detail, check out her website at www.zonya.com.

Drink water... *and think before you drink anything else.*

Include breakfast... *and stop eating two to three hours before bedtime.*

Eat often... *and include a fruit or vegetable each time.*

Tame your sweet tooth... **and naturally eat as little sugar as possible.**
> Eat a piece of fruit, drink a glass of water and then eat half of that treat. Limit to two treats/day.

Find the fat... *and know the good, the bad and the ugly.*

Replace processed food with wholesome... *and shop natural, close-to the-farm*

Eat until no longer hungry... *and stop the lead-filled beach ball!*

Every day exercise... *and make it your middle name.*

Further, she says, "Every once in awhile, when the urge or circumstance dictates, it's OK to live outside the guidelines of these habits. That's because this isn't a diet. This is DIET FREE! And if any one of the habits ever begins to feel like a diet, then it becomes worthless!" In other words, treat yourself!

LAUGHTER and PLAY

> Life has a way of sending us pop quizzes. A well-exercised sense of humor helps us succeed while maintaining our humanity, sanity, and dignity.

Laughter as a survival tool is just plain good science. Among its benefits are:

- Laughter stimulates physical healing.
- It enhances our creativity.
- It is good for relationships.
- It's good exercise: one minute of laughter is equal to 10 minutes on a rowing machine (Dr. William Fry, Stanford University).

- Laughter releases endorphins, which elevate mood and relieves pain
- Mirthful laughter creates eustress -- a state that produces healthy or positive emotions (Dr. Lee Berk and Dr. Stanley Tan, of Loma Linda).
- It activates the immune system by increasing the number and activity level of natural killer cells, T lymphocytes, IgA, Igb and Complement 3, all of which attack virus infected cells and some types of cancer and tumor cells.
- "It reduces hostility, deflects criticism, relieves tension, improves morale, and helps communicate difficult messages" (Salo Fabio, Harvard Business Review).

Play as a survival tool is good science. Every species learns and maximizes tool use through play, and learns to stretch boundaries. This gives them an adaptive edge.

Laughter as a survival tool is just plain good business.

- Work- and industry-related studies have found that *productivity* of factory workers increased after they viewed funny movies.
- "Those who feel their work is fun perform better and *get along better* with co-workers than those who were satisfied with their jobs but didn't see them as fun" (David Abramis, in Leigh, Edward. Making Work Fun).
- People who had just seen a funny movie had *"creative flexibility"* as opposed to "functional fixedness" (Dr. Alice Isen, Cornell University).

Case in point: many of us geezers fear that the joystick is a step backward in individual intelligence and social progress, but consider the following:

- » The military is in the game business in both their recruitment and training. We have long been aware of the use of simulation exercise in aeronautics.

» Research has found that physicians who spent at least three hours each week with video games made 37 percent fewer mistakes in laparoscopies and were 27 percent faster.

» Playing video games enhances the ability to detect changes in the environment and the ability to process multiple sources of information simultaneously.

» Experiences with these simulation games can deepen the aptitude of empathy and offer rehearsals for the social interactions of our lives

Perhaps joysticks and video games are not the beginning of the end but rather a vital tool for our future. We just need to be vigilant and provide opportunities to balance this type of activity with real social interaction. As with anything, you can get too much of a good thing, *so practice moderation.*

Play at Work

Steve Wilson introduces the art of mixing work and play in his book *PWLOARYK*. Author/speaker Sheila Feigelson gives you concrete skills to *Energize Your Meetings With Laughter*. Research started in the 1950s, proved that people who have fun and enjoy their work are more productive, creative and satisfied.

For another take on this, Kahlil Gibran writes, "If you cannot work with love but only with distaste, it is better that you should leave your work and sit at the gate of the temple and take alms of those who work with joy." This may seem extreme, but I am living proof of survival when thrown out on my own. I did in fact love my job and did not quit of my own volition. But when I was laid off for the second time in two years, I must admit, I could see nothing but distaste in the idea of shackling myself again to an 8-5, Monday -- Friday noose that required that I go to meetings, supervise people and manage a million dollar budget. Hence, I set out on my own, and I've now been self-employed longer than I ever held any job.

Laughter How-to's:

Laughter and play get stifled when we think too much and try to control behavior to the degree that our Puritan work ethic dictates. Laughter is a natural, spontaneous human expression. More than that, some versions of yoga have always included the practice of laughter. Five minutes of laughter early in the morning is said to be equal to eight hours of zazen, their deepest form of meditation. This is easier said than done. Have you ever tried to laugh for five minutes? Especially early in the morning, while your system is still figuring which end is up?

> "Laughter captures a moment of joy and emphasizes the divine in all of us."

Ideas to help you add more laughter to your life

Join a yogic Laughter Club – laugh for no reason.
> These are cropping up all over the world. Go to laughteryoga.org to find a club near you.

Check out Laughter tracks (tapes or CDs …you could do this in your car).

Laughter with play works best for me…..
> A friend of mine used to bat a beachball back and forth with his daughter every morning, until she "got too old for that sort of thing." The laughter came naturally.

Check out: Youtube – laughing meditation.

Try Centered Silliness: The Laughing Meditation exercise (Exercise 6.2).

Add your own:

_____

_____

_____

EXERCISE 6.2 CENTERED SILLINESS
LAUGHING MEDITATION/MINDFUL LAUGHING

Adapted from: Dailyom.com, September 16, 2005,

Many people might be surprised to think of laughter as a form of meditation. Yet laughing is not only meditation but one of the simplest forms of meditation. And a very powerful one. The physical act of laughing is one of the few actions involving the body, the emotions and the soul. When we laugh, we give ourselves over to the immediacy of the present moment. We also

Continued on next page...

Exercise 6.2 Centered Silliness
Laughing Meditation/Mindful Laughing (continued)

are able to momentarily transcend minor physical and mental stresses. Practiced in the morning, laughing meditation can lend a joyful quality to the entire day. Practiced in the evening, laughing meditation is a potent relaxant that has been known to inspire pleasant dreams. Laughter also can help open our eyes to previously unnoticed absurdities that can make life seem less serious.

There are three stages to mindful laughter. Each stage can last anywhere from 5 to 20 minutes.

1.) The first stage involves stretching your body like a cat and breathing deeply. Your stretch should start at the hands and feet. Then, feel the stretch move through the rest of your body. Stretch out the muscles in your face by yawning and making silly faces.

2.) The second stage of the meditation is pure laughter. Imagine a humorous situation, remember funny jokes, or think about how odd it is to be laughing by yourself. When the giggles start to rise, let them. Let the laughter ripple through your belly and down into the soles of your feet. Let the laughter lead to physical movement. Roll on the floor if you have to, and keep on laughing until you stop.

3.) The final stage of the meditation is one of silence. Sit with your eyes closed and become aware of your breath. Feel the cooling of your nostrils and the expansion of your belly as you inhale. Feel the warming of your nostrils and the deflation of your belly as you exhale.

Laughter brings with it a host of positive effects that operate on both the physical and mental levels. It is also fun, and expressive, and a way to release tension. Learn to laugh in the present moment, and you'll find that joy is always there.

Laughter Bites

- The average adult laughs about 15 times/day.
- The average person has approximately the same number of anger episodes/day.
- Children laugh 500 times/day.
- We rarely laugh alone.
    - » In the 1930s and 1940s, at the Ford Motor Company's River Rouge plant, laughter was a disciplinary offense, and humming, whistling and smiling were evidence of insubordination. (David Collinson)
    - » "The opposite of play isn't work. It's depression" (Brian Sutton-Smith, University of Pennsylvania).
    - » More than 50 European companies brought in consultants in "serious play", who used Lego building blocks to train corporate executives. British Airways has hired its own "corporate jester" (Wall Street Journal).
    - » "In the Conceptual Age...fun and games are not just fun and games—and laughter is no laughing matter" (Daniel Pink). Laughter and play enhance the right brain's ability to solve problems that require pattern recognition: spotting trends, drawing connections, discerning the big picture.

What's Funny?

- When another person uses humor *with* you.
- When you have a strong relationship with the other person.
- When the situation is socially appropriate (party vs. funeral...though sometimes it's even appropriate there).
- When you use humor aimed at yourself.
- When you use humor to poke fun at a situation.
  (not at another person or group of persons that would be unhealthy humor).

What's Not Funny?
Hurtful humor creates pain & distance

- Humor that pokes fun at individuals or groups, even if you yourself are part of that group
- Sarcasm, put-downs, ethnic jokes, anti jokes (anti-men, anti-women, ethnicities).
- Ridicule – jesting words, caricature, mocking, slightly contemptuous laughter.
- "Pulling your leg," "giving you a hard time" is poking fun at someone or something. Even the toughest of tough-skinned-people can be hurt on an off-day.
- Tickling is invading personal space and can be painful for some people – listen to "no" or "stop."

Negative humor can be destructive. It can reflect and reinforce, articulate and highlight workplace divisions, tensions, conflicts, power asymmetries and inequalities" (David L. Collinson).

Play Bites

"I play with ideas."

Einstein

"You can discover more about a person in an hour of play than in a year of conversation."

Plato

"[Humankind] does not cease to play because it grows old; it grows old because it ceases to play."

George Bernard Shaw

VOLUNTEERING

My thoughts on volunteering, while brief, are heartfelt. If you are lonely, if you are depressed, if your job is unfulfilling, your life is unbalanced. Volunteering will help reestablish balance. Your job does not owe it to you to fulfill all the needs of your life.

English author Arnold Bennett says it well: "The best cure for worry, depression, melancholy, brooding, is to go deliberately forth and try to lift with one's sympathy the gloom of somebody else." So get out and volunteer. Volunteer in a position where you will have contact with the people in need. I have heard it said that to look into the face of another is to see the divine.

Volunteering takes you outside of yourself, allowing you to walk in someone else's shoes, to learn compassion and gratitude. It may be a formal volunteer job or as simple as looking out for an elderly neighbor.

STRONG EMOTIONAL REACTIONS

Brian Luke Seaward defines emotional well-being as "the ability to feel and express the full range of human emotions and to control these feelings, not be controlled by them." Balance.

By practicing meditation, stress management and a healthy amount of self-analysis (not flagellating ourselves, but being realistic and practicing moderation), we can learn to manage and control our emotions. I will have to say that having finally arrived on the other side of that women's milestone, menopause. I am so grateful not to have the emotional swings of my younger years. Men, you cannot possibly imagine! If these self-help remedies do not help, seeking professional assistance may be indicated.

> Control your emotions...don't let them control you

Confrontation has always been difficult for me. In my earlier years, I did find that when I was feeling upset or confrontational, I needed to check when my period was due. It's not that there weren't issues that needed resolving, but rather, if I could afford to wait, I would be less emotional. And I could make a clearer case when I chose to confront someone.

> ### EXERCISE 6.3 STORMY WEATHER – JOURNALING
>
> When rough times hit, when there is angst at home or at work, or anytime when you have a strong emotional reaction, journal.
>
> Ask yourself: How am I contributing to this storm?
>
> How can I act differently?
>
> How might the other party(s) react to this?
>
> How will I maintain my balance?
>
> If you have an issue like this in your life, take the time to do this exercise now.
>
> _____
>
> _____

A Note about Tears

It has been found that tears of joy have a different chemical make-up than tears of grief. Emotional tears are unique to humans. They are one of three types of tears: basal tears, for lubrication; irritant tears which have chemicals and antimicrobials in them; and emotional tears. Emotional tears contain hormones and natural painkillers that increase when we are under emotional stress. Prolactin and ACTH, major stress hormones, are significantly higher in the bloodstream and in emotional tears when we are under stress. Prolactin is a hormone that is much higher in women. And not surprisingly, women cry more often than men.

In other words, crying rebalances the system and releases toxic stress hormones. Many report feeling better after a well-timed cry. An additional evolutionary significance may be that many times crying can bring people together (William Frey).

EXERCISE 6.4   YAH-BUT REVISITED

Compile a list of some of the changes you'd like to make in your life and what's keeping you from realizing them. Apply it to:

Laughter _____

_____

Play _____

_____

Nutrition _____

_____

Exercise _____

_____

Simplicity _____

_____

Enoughness _____

_____

Time management _____

Continued on next page...

EXERCISE 6.4 YAH-BUT REVISITED (CONTINUED)

Money management _____

_____

Ex.: I like to play board games, but there are only two of us in the family and it's not as much fun with two as with more players.

> I'd like to spend more time with my family, but I travel a lot for my job.

Exchange "and" for "but." And move from excuse-making into problem-solving mode.

D. Pink: A Whole New Mind

See also, Ex. 3.1

SECTION III

RELATIONSHIPS

> **Three Grand Essentials of Happiness**
>
> Something to do
> Something to love
> Something to hope for
>
> *Allan Chalmersand*

OF SPECIAL NOTE......

We are social beings. We need one another.

I had never given this any concentrated thought until I was in my late 30s and dating again. I felt foolish for having my spirits rise when I heard Steve's voice on the answering machine. I mentioned this to my minister one day, and his response made me realize that we truly are interconnected. It's not being needy but merely being human.

While it is the human condition that we appear separate, it is human nature to need other people, to feel connected. As further proof of this inherent quality, I need only remember Marilyn. She was 89 when I met her at the nursing home where I brought my nurse aide students. I worked with her for three years, and every time one of us told her that we would wheel her down to the dining room, she would take our hand in both of hers and look closely into our face as she spoke. Invariably she said, "Oh, your hands are so warm," and she would bring our hand to her check and just hold it there. You knew that it was the warmth of human touch she was cherishing. Then, when you had settled her into her recliner after the meal, she would ask for her blanket and her bear. It was one of those 2-foot, super-soft, scrunchy bears, and she would put both arms around it and curl into it. It was one of the most endearing sights I and my students had ever seen. For her, it was connection and comfort. We need one another.

Suffering is ego's illusion that we are separate, limited, powerless and isolated. There was a television show in the '70s called *One Day At A Time*. I remember my mother enjoying it. She remarked that it was the first time she had ever felt there were others with similar life experiences. It was about a single mom with two teen-aged girls;

while my mother was married and had four teen-aged girls. But it was one of the first shows depicting home life as it really was, not the Ozzie and Harriet or the Dick VanDyke Show fantasy. Life had hit my mother hard, and she suffered severe bouts of depression over at least 20 years. This comment gave me a glimpse of her isolation and loneliness. My mother felt different from her neighbors on many levels: education, religion, and we were from Boston, living in a small Midwest community in the '60s. These were barriers that my mother never learned to break through effectively. Her comment is a lesson I have never forgotten. When reaching out to comfort, the connection of similar experience is a profound one.

Failure to thrive is a condition characterized by apathy, poor weight gain, or weight loss and general decline. It was originally identified in newborn monkeys and used to describe a condition in infants who have not bonded with another human being and fail to gain weight, fail to thrive. Now it is also used as a diagnosis in hospice for a state of decline in the very old. But what about the years in between infancy and old age? Is our need for connection any less? Where does this phenomenon go in those in-between years? I would challenge us to consider that it does not disappear -- it merely goes underground. The sheer volume and momentum of routine activities may keep us going in those years, but it may just be subsistence living. Why is depression in pandemic proportions? Not to mention all the self-defeating behaviors we practice, from fast food and french fries to alcohol, gambling, spending, and tobacco -- behaviors that fill a void, that give a temporary rush, that numb the feelings of isolation, loneliness, and depression.

Henry Grayson tells us relationships can be heaven or hell. Or degrees of both. "The end of suffering and the advent of joyful relationships will come from an awareness of who and what we truly are and embracing this godlike essence that we all possess—each and every one of us. If we insist on believing in the common illusions that we are powerless and separate, then we will continue to be at the mercy of our relationships." Instead, recognize the interconnectedness and become the "master of how you feel in your relationships, letting them flow from an endless supply of love. With this shift in thinking, you will know to ask yourself, "'How am I contributing to this storm?'

With this new awareness you can learn both how to quell the storms of your relationship and how to stay centered, in spite of those storms" (*Mindful Loving*).

Iyanla Vanzant says, "All relationships are healing opportunities." They provide us with an opportunity, a practice ground, to learn new information with which to heal our hearts and minds. She goes on to say, "Those who agree to have a relationship with us, love us enough to spend some part of their lives in our healing process." This only makes sense. We cannot learn in a vacuum. If there is nothing to challenge our status quo, we are less likely to even consider change. It is through the friction of human interaction that we learn and grow. Through this process some of our rougher edges, our near-sightedness, our uncompromising attitudes, our less compassionate nature become exposed to ourselves and we face a choice: growth or stagnation.

Friendships need to be tended carefully and maintained with love. As do work relationships, social relationships and family relationships. The following sections will explore our relationship with self; with friends, family members and significant others; with our relationships at work; and with the divine.

Chapter 7
RELATIONSHIP WITH SELF
Being…..Happy and Whole

> **Look within for happiness**
> **Look outward for companionship**

First things first: you must take care of yourself. You have to get things right with yourself, or there's nothing for anyone else. As Thich Nhat Hanh states, you must "restore peace within yourself, restore harmony and order to your body, honor your body." Take care of yourself, accept yourself. The Buddha says, "The object of your practice should first of all be yourself. Your love for the other, your ability to love another person, depends on your ability to love yourself". And Jesus told us to "love your neighbor as yourself" (Mark 12:31). Do the math. Love of self has to come first.

So attend to nutrition, exercise, time management, money management, sleep, laughter and play. Your body needs all of these in balance to optimize happiness. On another level, self-care includes spending time with your elf, liking yourself. It is about being happy and whole, whether you are single or in a committed relationship.

There is a difference between being alone and being lonely. Being alone can be a good thing. In our go - go - go society, being still and alone are foreign and sometimes frightening concepts. It takes time and practice to get comfortable in that space. I have gone through this transition at least a dozen times over the past 20 years, where life was what I called crazy-busy and then would get very slow and quiet. It feels unnatural at first, with those voices inside saying "You should be doing something; if you're not, something is wrong." I have to tell myself to breathe, that this is a good thing and it will feel natural again soon. This is a very important space to cultivate, because "happiness arises in a state of peace, not of tumult" (Ann Radcliffe, *The Mysteries of Udolpho*).

We have all had times in the midst of relationships when we felt cold, lost and depressed. Even when involved in a busy family life, one can still be lonely. Loneliness in this space can be extremely painful -- all of our past learning tells us this isn't the way it is supposed to work. This only compounds the feeling of isolation and loneliness. The books *Mindful Loving* by Henry Grayson and *The Dance of Intimacy* by Harriet Goldher-Lerner are very helpful resources at such times. My personal struggle with loneliness went on for five to six years as I tried various strategies to reattach with my husband. I tried individual counseling, marriage counseling, attending Co-Dependents Anonymous (for those people at least one generation away from addiction; my father and husband were both adult children of alcoholics). In the attempt to reconnect with my husband, I contemplated dressing in saran wrap or whipped cream to greet him coming home, but somehow that felt hollow. Lerner's book came out toward the end of this experience. With its insights, I was finally able to put some distance between me and the issues and not be the "chaser." I was no longer enmeshed and entangled. I was non-judgmental and non-reactive about whether he loved me enough. Perversely, or in consequence as Ms. Lerner purports, he became more attentive. Before the rebirth of the relationship became firmly established, however the opportunity was lost when I moved home to care for my terminally ill mother. The fragile bond did not withstand the separation.

It is an illusion that we are separate, that we are incomplete. Because of this common belief that we are incomplete, we tend to view love as a commodity -- something outside of ourselves, according to Grayson. So we look for the love we want from others, rather than understanding that we already *are* the love we are searching for. We *are* love and have an infinite supply of it. Seeking love implies that we believe we are separate from it. Anytime we feel a need for love, all we need to do is to extend it and we will experience love — inside of us, not separate from us. An additional benefit of this framework is that we no longer feel or appear needy. As a profound example of this, I took on two high-school foreign exchange students -- more life and a chance to offer love freely. One month later, I met a lovely man and am in a relationship for the first time in 15 years. I embraced life, and life happened.

Staying single is a choice, whether you're widowed, divorced or never married. Likewise, living alone is a choice. It may be semantics, but there were and are choices. Claiming it as a choice, leads to an attitude change, which can make a tremendous difference in your happiness. Researchers are finding what some of us may have learned intuitively: when you can't change a circumstance, you adapt and become happy with what you have. You can be alone without being lonely. It is not just making do, it is happiness.

Being single, one has greater opportunity to decide the when, where, who, and how of your relationships. Even if there is a "special person" who rejects you, you can choose to wallow in your feelings, or choose to move on. Accept that it was not meant to be, that there is a relationship better suited to you out there. That special relationship may take the form of people you assist through volunteer work, it may be a pet, or it may even be a child whom you adopt. You need to be willing to think outside the box that says the only way to happiness is romance, marriage, children, house and a two-car garage. Happiness does not necessarily come in that package.

The solution remains the same, whether you're single or attached: first love yourself, then give love. Anything else, after all, is secondhand. There is no question that sharing moments of joy and happiness with another person increases the intensity of that joy. Having friends and companions to share time and experiences with is valuable and creates a holistic, healthy lifestyle.

Chapter 8
RELATIONSHIP WITH THE DIVINE

> "We are not human beings on a spiritual journey, we are spiritual beings on a human journey."
>
> *Stephen R. Covey*

"We are not human beings on a spiritual journey, we are spiritual beings on a human journey" (Stephen R. Covey).

To be truly happy, we need to be mindful of this spiritual dimension. We need to develop a purpose in life. We need to love and be compassionate, to forgive, take time to enjoy nature and the mysteries of life. Be mindful. Practice being in our sanctuary.

M. Scott Peck theorized four stages of human spiritual development in his book *Further Along the Road Less Traveled: The Unending Journey Toward Spiritual Growth*. These stages provide a useful paradigm to understand our spiritual development, as well as what is in store for us next.

Stage 1 is the chaotic, disordered and reckless individual. He has an undeveloped spirituality, even absence or bankruptcy of spirit. Young children are in stage 1 by virtue of their immaturity, as well as adults whose lives are in chaos because of addictions, codependency or a helpless-hopeless attitude. Those adults are characterized by a poor self-relationship, poor self-awareness, poor relationships and a weak value system. They have unresolved conflicts and lack a meaningful purpose in life. Criminals often are in this stage of development, and Peck further contends that evil people will attack others rather than face their own failures (*The Road Less Traveled*).

Stage 2 is the formal-institutional individual – the person who has a blind faith in institutions that provide rules and structure. She is looking for her personal needs to be met and for life's answers to be handed to her. Unmet needs at this stage lead to a regression to stage 1.

Stage 3 is the scientific, skeptical individual who begins to question the truths that institutions represent. Though these people are looking for truth, they don't accept things on faith -- they must be logically convinced.

Stage 4 is the mystic-communal individual who starts enjoying the mystery of nature and existence. She seeks out continuing challenges, looking for clues and answers. Relationships, connection and community factor in greatly. Here the individual loves others as herself, decreases attachment to ego and forgives enemies. Working among mankind, such individuals create "love where love did not exist" (*The Road Less Traveled*).

Putting Spirituality into Practice

Revisit what you wrote in Exercises 2.1 and 2.2, "What Animates Your Life" and "Guiding Principles." Tweak them, revisit them periodically, post them on notecards if you haven't already.

Chapter 9
FAMILY RELATIONSHIPS

> Communication not only is the lifeblood of love and the guarantee of its growth, but is the very essence of love in practice.
>
> <u>The Secret of Staying in Love</u>, John Powell, S.J.

> In every dispute between parent and child, both cannot be right, but they may be, and usually are, both wrong. It is this situation which gives family life its peculiar hysterical charm.
>
> Isaac Rosenfeld

My family has always ascribed to the adage "Distance makes the heart grow fonder." There is wisdom in the saying because familiarity can indeed breed contempt. Even with someone for whom we have unconditional love, we sometimes find ourselves impatient or sarcastic. We get busy and may think we understand the issue at hand, but chances are, we are just familiar with it and our loved one's reaction, and have not truly taken the time to understand. For if we had taken the time to understand, we would feel awe and compassion. Mature understanding breeds compassion.

Love in a committed relationship that results in lasting happiness is a decision: unconditional love and support through the journey of life. It really is not any different from love within the family. Loving kindness, compassion, joy and freedom are all essential elements. Being there for the loved one, through joy and suffering, is what it is all about. But there are additional issues that need to be managed when two become three or more. Whether it is adult members or children being added, additional tools are needed such as discipline and family meetings to facilitate smooth operations.

Discipline

The following is not intended to be a primer on discipline. And I use the word "discipline" loosely. If the term "solutions" works better for you, please substitute that whenever you read "discipline." Don't get caught up in the semantics. These are a few of the techniques I have found effective and some resources to use to start your quest to find what works for you and your family. Even though the form of the discipline will be different for each family and even each child, the basic premise remains the same: children need structure, and they need to be protected from unsafe personal discovery. For the child who persists in running out in the street without looking, solutions need to be found, and quickly.

Some General Principles

- » Encouragement helps children feel that they belong; spend special time being with them -- tuck them into bed and share your day; tell a story; give children meaningful jobs; involve them in volunteer work for an elderly neighbor or a friend.
- » Teach and model mutual respect. Teach children about cooling-off periods. It is best for both of you to take a time-out. Physical separation is good (go to another room), so you both can come back to the issue without heat and with mutual respect.
- » Remember that it takes a village to raise a child (ancient African proverb) – church, school, neighborhood, family. (I cannot bake to save my life, but my daughter enjoys it. So I farmed her out to Donnis from our church to teach her how to make a pie. They had a great time and I reaped the benefits!)
- » Anne Wilson Schaef shares a daily reflection on raising children in her book *Native Wisdom for White Minds*, stating, "Control does not support growth. We need to find ways to give our children freedom and safety," and quotes Rangimarie Turuki Pere, a Maori writer: "In general, children were encouraged to explore and use their environment to

learn and discover things for themselves. They were told and shown the places declared tapu [taboo] for them, such as dangerous river holes, cliff faces, swamps, reefs, in fact anything that could be too difficult for them to cope with unless accompanied by adults."

» Discipline needs to be matched to the child and situation. For example, I sent my 10-year-old daughter to her bedroom to eat dinner once (my parents had done it to me many times). It devastated her. I never did that again. On the other hand, when she was 13, upset and winding herself up, I sent her to her room until she could control herself. She thanked me for it afterwards. Emotional self-control is one of the most helpful skills we can teach our children.

» Keep discipline one-on-one as much as possible. Let the children "save face" this way. Otherwise it adds humiliation into the picture, which is less a less healthy, more manipulative form of discipline.

» Brainstorming discipline solutions - Use the three R's and an H for solutions: related, respectful, reasonable and helpful, from the *Positive Discipline* series by Jane Nelson. Related: the solution needs to be a logical match. When my daughter was winding up, time alone to wind down was logical. Respectful – no shouting, no physical pain or insults, etc. Reasonable – until she could be calm again. Helpful – at 10 years of age, including dinner, it did not work. When she was older and the situation matched, it worked and was helpful.

> In dwelling, live close to the ground.
> In thinking, keep to the simple.
> In conflict, be fair and generous.
> In governing, don't try to control.
> In work, do what you enjoy.
> In family life, be completely present.
>
> *Tao Te Ching*

Logical Consequences

While raising my daughter, I found that an ounce of prevention worked for me because it prevented my angst. Therefore, when there was a repetitive behavior that I found myself nagging her about (chores, cleaning her room), I used a behavior modification technique. I used this technique for about five years, between the ages of 5 and 9. I stapled a sturdy piece of cloth to a piece of cardboard and cut four rows of seven slits, one for each day of the week and four weeks (similar to those coin saving cards that churches give out at Christmas time and Lent). Each night if she did her chores without me nagging, or behaved, or whatever the issue was at the time, we put in a nickel, and when she was older, a dime into the pocket for that day. At the end of the week, she got the coins. This uses the four R's in establishing logical consequences (relevant, respectful, reasonable and revealed in advance). You want to be careful not to disguise punishment as a logical consequence. What you really want is the behavior to stop and the child to learn self-discipline in the process.

Variations of this can be used to teach delayed gratification: don't give them the coins at the end of the week, instead when they reach a certain number such as seven or ten coins, etc. Or when they have mastered the task: seven in a row, they get all the coins.

The Power of 1-2-3

When you have told a child to do or stop doing something and he continues to protest or procrastinate, I have always found that counting to three out loud with a logical consequence attached if he doesn't comply works wonders. I have even used it silently across a noisy public pool by raising my hand and putting up fingers. I have also bent the rules and been known to count: 1, 2, 2 ½, 2 5/8, 2 ¾, as the child reluctantly starts moving. Using it consistently is the key, along with not backing off from the consequences.

Too Funny

Having had only one child, I had never had to deal with the "You love her better than me" game. Last year I had two foreign exchange students, Gabby who turned 16 while she was here (I had her for nine months), and Chris, who was 18 (I had her for the last four months). Chris was complaining because Gabby was able to stay overnight every weekend lately and somehow I apparently was asking her to do something that I wasn't asking of Gabby. Discussing it in the car, Chris pulls out the age-old saying, "You love Gabby more than me -- she's been here longer." I was so proud of myself for being able to respond immediately (probably because I didn't have the heat of a long history with these two). "I love you just as much. I could take the easy route and do things the same with you two, but you are individuals and need different things. If I loved you less, I would do the same, instead I am making my decision based on what YOU need. Because I love you." I surprised myself with the quickness of my response. Though this example is about privileges, not discipline, the correlation is clear: tailor the solutions to the child. Refuse to play the favorites/victim game.

EXERCISE 9.1 THE POWWOW FAMILY MEETING GUIDELINES

The family meeting has simple guidelines. The key to success is commitment and flexibility. Modify these guidelines to fit your family's style.

1. As much as possible, the family meeting is held at a regularly scheduled time and day of the week. The family decides the length of meetings -- often a half hour for families with small children, a little longer for families with older children or teenagers.

Continued on next page...

Exercise 9.1 The Powwow (continued)

2. It is better if everyone agrees to take part, but it can be held even when a member of the family cannot or will not participate. Issues are discussed by the whole family. Simply knowing that you have a forum at which to discuss things can help smooth out problems even as they come up during the week.

3. The meeting:

    a) The leader starts every meeting with compliments (give roses or balloons, etc.). Bring popcorn or freshly baked brownies. Do a family meditation (mindful breathing exercise) and/or prayer.

    b) Issues: the leader asks if anyone has any issues to discuss. These can be things such as, "People need to put the toilet seat down" to "how are we going to try to be more frugal this Christmas?"

    c) Third on the agenda is family play date – A time when the whole family does things together. Discus what do we want to do on family play date? Each person comes up with a suggestion, and after that, use a process of discussion until there is general agreement (not majority rules). One way is to take a poll, narrow it down to a few options. Everyone has to agree to the final decision — if someone doesn't agree, a compromise or an alternate solution is discussed that makes everyone happy. Sometimes the solution is that, this week we'll do this, next week the other.

    d) Last is the fun thing. The leader gets to choose a fun thing to do to end the family meeting. This can be anything from taking turns adding to a short story and then reading out loud the wacky short story that results, an obstacle course race, a scavenger hunt, etc. Non-Competitive games are best. (Check out my game *Cartwheels®* for more ideas.)

Continued on next page...

Exercise 9.1   The Powwow (continued)

Note: Decisions are by consensus whenever possible; brainstorming all possible solutions is a good technique for avoiding parental edicts. Also, you may want to rearrange things, depending on everyone's mood -- put family day second or the fun thing first, etc.

Adapted from: http://www.familyeducationcenter.com/Fmeetings.htm and http://zenhabits.net/2007/02/family-day-and-family-meetings/

ACTION PLAN:

1. Set up your first powwow.
2. Set up your next family play date.
3. Meditation...make it a family affair.

NOTE: Changing the rules and adopting new strategies can be challenging and family members may resist. Be assertive. Introduce the powwows or family play dates by saying something like: "What we're doing is no longer working well for us. We need to try new strategies and find out what might work better for us. It will feel awkward at first, but let's explore and give each method a good try. It will not necessarily be easy at first, but it will get easier and it will be worth it."

Chapter 10
RELATIONSHIPS AT WORK

> "Let your life speak"
> *Quaker Proverb*

Negative energy saps your strength, squelches creativity, increases anger, frustration and irritability, and decreases job satisfaction. I have worked with mostly women all my life and have periodically held what I fondly call "Come to Jesus meetings" with my staff members. I had thought that with my nursing students, whom I have for just one day/week for 12 to16 weeks, that these would never be necessary, because we are together for barely three weeks. I have concluded that whining and complaining are the fight-or-flight manifestations of the 21st century. It is no longer acceptable to chop off the head of whoever disagrees with you, nor is it acceptable to turn and run, so the more subtle whining and complaining have taken their place.

One memorable semester, seven out of 10 students were actively demonstrating rampant negativity. After this semester, I instituted an oath that my students now take within 30 minutes of meeting me. They all take a chocolate in their upraised hands and repeat after me: "On my honor, to God, my country and fellow nursing students, I will not whine, I will not cry, and I will not gnash my teeth, no matter how many unexpected busy-work assignments, no matter how stressed by other classes and commitments. Should I feel the need to whine, to cry or to gnash my teeth, I will ask for chocolate or a tai chi or yoga moment." Then, if the students agree to the terms, they seal it by eating the chocolate. This has worked for me now for a number of semesters, until one notorious semester when it did not. So we had a come to Jesus meeting.

We had spent four weeks working on violence prevention strategies materials to use with a group of high-risk children. We were excited, and our expectations were high. Then the long awaited day arrived, and disappointment was rampant. There were small numbers of students. Not only that, but they looked and acted like normal kids. I had been touching base with all of my students throughout the day and so was unprepared for the brick wall that hit me in our postconference. Sidney was sitting across from me and started the discussion, complaining. The smallness of the groups, the kids were normal, she had spent so much time working on the lesson plans and it was all a waste, this is the wrong topic, the teacher felt it was a waste of time, and on and on and on and on. The energy went from Sidney to Georgia, who was on my right, who began to talk in the same negative vein: waste of time, wrong topic, there was so much disparity in the students' ages. Where Georgia left off, Loren on my other side started right in with the same negative spiel.

Mind-numbing, energy-sapping negativity. It is contagious. It feeds off itself and has a life of its own, causing a ripple effect on all those around you. It sucks people in and sucks them dry. Some people respond to a lesser degree. Some can stand firm, but it still shakes the positive energy of the entire group. It threatens everyone's ability to function, and it takes real effort for positive energy to reestablish itself.

In my come to Jesus meeting, I described what happened in terms of an energy field and its effect on the people involved. I went on to point out that each person has the power to choose effective stress management techniques or negative energy/whining and complaining and the ability to turn the working environment into what he/she wants it to be. Sometimes, going with the flow (of energy) is not the right decision -- it's just the easiest.

And thanks to feedback from my fall 2009 students, over the succeeding two semesters, I honed my opening speech even more. Kudos to my spring 2010 and 2011 groups (you know who you are). I have also added a new introduction that I use with this class, based on the Framingham study that found our happiness is affected by people three points removed from us.

In Your Relations at Work: Do the right thing

When I began practicing quality improvement and principle-centered leadership, I set out to create a non-co-dependent environment in my clinic operations. The authorities I had read said I couldn't do it without the support of the administration and the other divisions as well. But I could not just walk away. Neither could I keep going along with the status quo. If I was going to go down, I would go down doing the right thing. So I planted seeds, and progress was made.

It feels a little "out there" to be touting this type of administration in our daily business, but the simple fact is that if we keep doing what we've always done, can we really expect different results? "No one can deny the material benefits of modern life, but we are still faced with suffering, fear, and tension. [It's] only sensible to try to strike a balance between material development...and the development of spiritual value. [We need to make] our societies more compassionate, just, and equitable" [Dalai Lama *How To See Yourself As You Really Are*]. We spend at least one-third of our lives, nearly one-half of our waking lives at work -- how can we leave it out of the plan?

A Word on Bullying in the Workplace

What is it that makes bullies tick? Why is it that so many feel they must control those who work for them? Many practitioners have written of successful techniques that maintain dignity and respect yet still get the job done. But the rise in the number of approved worker's compensation clams related to workplace bullying attests to the fact that many bosses resort to bullying. I have several times over the years grappled with this issue as staffing changes made subtle changes in the groups' dynamics. Add to that the stressors from above (demands for increased productivity, budget cuts, etc.), and people tend to act out without thinking. Communication deteriorates and games proliferate, making for toxic or hostile work environments.

The following experts give us some insight into the largely unseen issue of workplace bullying.

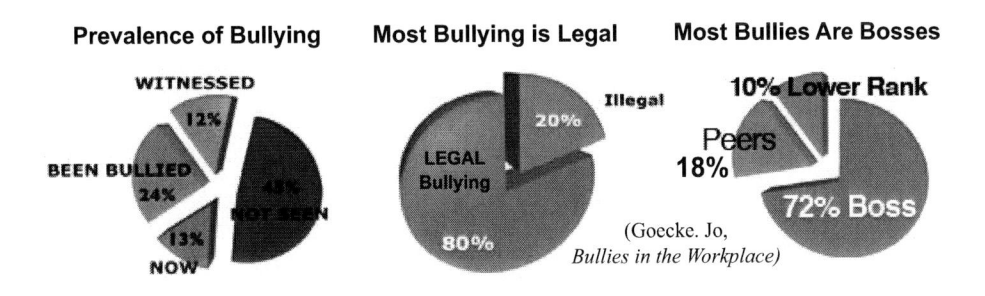

Prevalence of Bullying

WITNESSED 12%
BEEN BULLIED 24%
NOT SEEN 48%
NOW 13%

Most Bullying is Legal

Illegal 20%
LEGAL Bullying 80%

Most Bullies Are Bosses

10% Lower Rank
Peers 18%
72% Boss

(Goecke. Jo, *Bullies in the Workplace*)

The Stop Hate website tells us, "Never blame yourself for being bullied. The bully is the one with the problem. Being picked on by a bully does not make a person bad. Being tormented by a bully is not a sign of inner weakness. People who coped with bullying for years may have a high level of inner strength. Only a very weak person must use force, violence, insults or threats to manipulate people. A very tiny person makes others feel like trash to boost shallow self-esteem and to gain a sense of control."

Jo Goecke in his article "Bullies in the Workplace," states, "A common ploy used by bully managers to establish power and authority over their subordinates is to target the most vulnerable employees, then exploit them in front of others with excessive criticism, unfair reprimands, condescending directions and impossible deadlines. This public humiliation sends a strong message of intimidation to the victim's co-workers to conform or be targeted, too. When most employees have no job security and work long hours, it is a brutal control strategy that works."

Exercise 10.1 Be a Swan at Work

Envision a perfect workday. What would it look like? How would it start and end? How would it look, smell, sound, feel, taste? What would you choose to work on? Who would you choose to work with? Be as specific as you can be. This is your ideal workday.

Describe it. Include lunch, breaks, the physical environment.

What would you achieve? How would you treat people? How would people treat you?

_____

_____

_____

_____

_____

_____

_____

Dream it. How can you create it? What small things could YOU do today to move toward this ideal workday?

1. _____

2. _____

3. _____

Chapter 11

HOW TO STAY IN LOVE (PRACTICALLY) FOREVER

> "Keep talking and do fun/enjoyable/new things together."
>
> *Mom*

Healing Relationships: The Work of the Committed Relationship

I tend to carry the spirit of recycle and reuse to an extreme. My purple car died at the age of 13, having racked up 280,000 miles. The only thing that stopped it was being broadsided. My current car is 13, and had only 180,000 miles on it but it is still going strong. Of course, I pick well to start with, and I work at maintaining it. When I separated from my husband (who tended the cars), I had to become self-sufficient. So I did what I always do when I don't know something -- I bought a book: *Keep Your Car Running Practically Forever*.

So, first of all, I picked well; second, I researched it; and third, I worked at it. Religiously getting the oil changed every three months or 3,000 miles. Is it worth it? Yes. Even with nearly 300,000 miles on that purple car, repairs averaged less than $100/month, much lower than car payments. Each of my cars had a phase around 100,000 to 120,000 miles where a number of things went wrong. Then, just as I started wondering about cost and reliability, they started behaving.

> Love "is the essential component of human wholeness and happiness. To live is to love"
>
> *The Secret of Staying in Love*, John Powell, S.J.

The similarity to choosing and keeping a life partner is clear: pick well, research it, work at it, and have a strong commitment to withstand the challenges (at 120,000 miles, don't doubt him, just love him...it's just a phase). I have had several friends tell me, "It shouldn't be work." That's fiction. Tend the relationship lovingly, and when you are having a bad stretch, the unconditional love and support that you need will be there for you. In the words of Billy Joel, "tell her about it....you've got to provide communication constantly...Though you may not have done anything, will that be a consolation when she's gone." To give these guys some credit, I am sure they did not walk out the first time the relationship became work. But words do frame our reality. So perhaps saying "It shouldn't be suffering" would be healthier. Abuse and physical pain are different and need to be addressed (see Appendix 3). However, if the relationship *is* safe but becoming emotionally painful, take the time, get some counseling and give careful thought to where the pain is coming from. Is it truly being inflicted by the other person, or is it you exorcising ghosts? Painful as it might be, exorcising ghosts can be good and maybe even necessary for you to experience life fully, and give and receive love.

Growth * Healing * Joy

> To have happy and loving relationships is one of our deepest yearnings, and yet relationships are one of our greatest psychological and spiritual challenges.
>
> *Mindful Loving*

My staid church congregation had a good giggle when our minister, Lyle Heaton, once said, "Monks live together in monastic communities because it is the friction of living together that stimulates spiritual growth." The point is well made. "We need to flex and stretch, move against some form of resistance regularly" to grow and keep our spiritual muscles in good working order, (*Stressed is Desserts Spelled Backwards*). Relationships provide us with that forum. But a relationship can also be a scary place to be. You risk discovery and maybe even rejection and certainly, at times, the pain of exorcising ghosts.

Love in the Committed Relationship

To fully understand the dynamics in a committed relationship, it is useful to know that there are two major phases of love in committed relationships: the falling in love phase and the shared life journey.

> Love is an action word, not just an emotion

The falling in love phase generally lasts six to 24 months while the brain chemical phenylethylamine peaks and fades. When the chemical is released, we are ecstatic. It is a period of walking on air, of bonding and cleaving to each another. During what is often called the honeymoon phase, we idealize the other person, thinking only the best about him/her. It is a wonderful feeling, but it is fleeting. A dusty fact is that sexual attraction plays a huge part in this phase and is said to be 25 percent hormones and 75 percent imagination. By definition this phase/phenomenon is often about "me"" "*I* love her/him," "he/she loves *me*."

Henry Grayson, in *Mindful Loving*, discusses psychiatrist Wilhelm Reich's description of the falling-in-love syndrome as being a period of temporary psychosis. Grayson further states that in this phase, it is not the real person we relate to, but a projection of what we wish that person to be. We present our idealized self so that we never really meet each other at all. Too often we love the person for what we want from him/her. And when these unrealistic and inflated expectations go flat, the relationship goes bad -- we have created our own unhappiness. The ego self reestablishes itself, realizing that we are not one. The relationship either dissolves, or the work of real loving is initiated.

"We all know how to fall in love ...but not many of us know how to stay in love" (*Mental Resilience*). The emotions love and anger are polar opposites. If love is just an emotion, then you can't love your dog when it pees on the floor. Neither do we "fall in love" with our children in the traditional sense. Understanding the true nature of love, that it is not just an emotion resulting from following the inclinations of your hormones but a conscious decision, allows us to realize that we can love even when we don't feel like it. The practice of being there, of really seeing and hearing your loved one communicates love and keeps it fresh. Love is an action word, not just an emotion.

The second phase of love is the shared life journey. The main task is to give unconditional love and support through the journey of life. This is where the real relationship begins. There are couples who chose well at the outset. The one they fell in love with proved to be a good fit for their journey through life. Others of us did not discern between the dazzle of falling in love and the elements we needed in a life partner. Disappointment or anger erupts when the rose-colored glasses fall, resulting in many breakups within five years. Another way to explain this dynamic is in energy terms: if we are not whole in and of ourselves and we expect energy from another person to complete us, it can destroy the relationship.

> Harriet Lerner, in her book *The Dance of Connection*, tells us that intensity and intimacy are not the same thing. We need to ask ourselves:
>
> Is the relationship good for us? Are these elements present?
> - Conversation is safe and comfortable, making authenticity and self-disclosure possible.
> - My sense of self is enlarged with capacity to speak my own truths.
> - Mutuality, mutual respect, empathy, nurturance and caretaking are present.
> - We can voice our differences to bring conflict out in the open and resolve it.
>
> Note: Practice compassion and understanding.

Unconditional Love and Support: The Committed Relationship

Though there must be give and take in marriage, love must be given unconditionally for a healthy relationship. We need to take the time to listen and understand when our partner is in distress. When there is friction or tension, do not wait for the other to make the first move, even if you feel you are the one injured. There is no room for pride in the committed relationship.

This lesson was made clear to me the other day when my daughter came home from work upset because it had been *"days"* since she and her fiancé had talked, and today she had told him something three times over the telephone and he never once heard her. As a result, she didn't know what the plans were for the evening or even if he was picking her up. The doorbell was ringing simultaneous to this conversation, so as I went to answer the door, I left her with the thought: "What did you need to do to still have a good time this evening?" It was George at the door, her fiancé. I pushed him back out the door (yes, I really did push my future son-in-law out the door... backwards), handed him a pair of scissors and told him to cut some roses for her. As it turned out, he was just as frazzled and frustrated about the evening plans as my daughter. Reviewing events with them later, I asked what lessons they learned and they reported:

1. Laughter helps (mother's antics).
2. Communication (soon) is important.
3. Give roses, balloons, candy hearts (be the first). If you are feel-ing frazzled, your partner probably is, too.
4. And most important of all, sometimes you just do what your mother-in-law says, no questions, just do it (my son-in-law-to-be got extra points on this one, as he reported this lesson first).

Summary:
» Give love unconditionally, no strings attached.
» Know that a state of happiness is natural and right.
» Try not to judge or blame or criticize.
» Assume responsibility for your part in the world and your effect on it.

Peak Experiences versus Stagnation

John Powell says that a peak experience is where you become aware of something in your partner that you never before experienced. You become more aware of that person's depth and mystery. As a result, the whole relationship acquires a new depth and intensity, new perspective of each other. "Without these moments of breakthrough into new and mutual transparency, love becomes dull, stagnant and boring."

I have found this statement especially fascinating. When I first read it, I could identify a number of times when, even in friendships, I had felt elated and closer to friends after what started almost as confrontation but ended in understanding. Until I read John Powell's words, I did not believe it was healthy, and I didn't trust it.

It is obvious that to keep a relationship viable, we must communicate and we must risk opening ourselves to our partner. Like any skill, communication takes practice, and practice needs to occur daily. It takes two to communicate successfully. It takes courage to share, and it takes skill to listen. I say this because I am sorely afflicted with bilateral foot-in-mouth disease. Sometimes we just get it wrong; or we are heard wrong. Smooth, easy, healthy conversation will not magically happen when you fall in love. It cannot be banked. It must be practiced often.

> "To the extent that I communicate myself as a person to you and you communicate yourself to me, we share in common the mysteries of ourselves...the extent that we withdraw from each other and refuse mutual transparency, love is diminished"
>
> <u>The Secret of Staying in Love</u>, John Powell, S.J.

Tools for the Journey of Life

When entering a committed relationship, what you are actually preparing for is a journey, a journey of life with a partner. However adept at communication you may be yourself, now you need to learn the techniques/practices as a couple and as a family. Your skills are only one-third of the equation. An additional one-third is your partner's skills, and one-third is merging them, using them in synchronicity. Then you need to practice those skills routinely. Practice time may even need to be scheduled when life gets hectic (see Family Powwows).

The characteristics or spiritual muscles below are the experts' take on what will strengthen your ability to provide unconditional love and support. Just as you are the only person whom you can change, for you to feel love, love needs to come from you. The exercises below are the tools that will help you cultivate those characteristics.

Kamal Sarma contends that learning how to listen increases your ability to stay connected and enhances your relationships. With all the chatter going on in our heads, it is often difficult to focus on our partners. Practice listening – it heightens clarity and allows us to connect with our emotions and our partners. And further, "Practicing focus and clarity ensures that we keep love alive in our relationships" with improved listening skills and emotional awareness. He calls this mental resilience training.

Thich Nhat Hanh offers us four essential elements of love in his book *True Love*:

1.) *Loving-kindness and benevolence* is the desire *and the ability* to bring joy to the beloved person. It requires what he calls deep looking and time to understand the essence of the loved one's troubles and aspirations.

2.) *Compassion* is the desire and ability to ease the pain of the beloved. This requires knowledge and understanding, which are possible through practicing meditation and looking deeply.

3.) The third element is *joy*. If there is no joy, it is not true love. There should not be suffering all the time, making your loved one cry.

4.) And finally, there is *equanimity or freedom*. You bring freedom to the person you love, as well as to yourself. You ask, "Beloved, do you have enough space in your heart and all around you?"

Additionally, Thich Nhat Hanh spells out four mantras of true love. You may need to practice saying these, even if only to yourself, especially when life gets hectic and stressed:

(1) "Dear one, I am really here for you." Love is being there with your true presence. Mindful breathing is the practice that enhances this, allowing you to be fully present (See Ex. 11.2).

(2) "I know that you are here, and it makes me very happy." This is recognizing the presence of the other. Thich Nhat Hanh further states, "To love is to be; to be loved is to be recognized by the other."

(3) "I know that you are suffering, that is why I am here for you." Be there when your loved one is suffering.

(4) "Dear one, I am suffering, please help." Overcome your pride when you are suffering, even if you believe your suffering has been created by the one you love the most (often a misconception).

I Corinthians tells us the characteristics of love that spring from practicing true love: "Love is patient and kind, never jealous or envious, never boastful or proud, never haughty or selfish or rude. Love does not demand its own way, it is not irritable or touchy. It does not hold grudges and will hardly even notice when others do it wrong. It is never glad about injustice, but rejoices whenever truth wins out. If you love someone you will be loyal to him no matter what the cost. You will always believe in him, always expect the best of him, and always stand your ground in defending him" (I Corinthians 13:4 - 7, TLB). In other words, these are the characteristics of unconditional love and support.

> When we think a loving or compassionate thought,
> we have just exercised our power to create reality
> to create peace and joy in this, as in every relationship.

EXERCISE 11.1   CONSCIOUS LISTENING REVISITED

"You must practice deep looking" without judgment or comment to really understand this person. Without understanding, love is not possible. This takes time, being attentive, observant and you must look deeply. Seek understanding. "The practice of understanding is the practice of meditation"…to look deeply into the heart of things.

<u>True Love</u>, Thich Nhat Hanh

<u>Listening exercise</u>

- » Choose a quiet, comfortable place and turn off all distractions.
- » With your partner, identify who is the speaker and who is the listener
- » The listener's role is just to listen, without comment or judgment
- » Start with 1 to 2 minutes of mindful breathing (Exercise 11.4).
- » Deep, attentive listening, is a meditation….maintain calm.
- » Be actively compassionate.
- » Listen with calmness and understanding, always nonjudgmental.
- » Just listen for an hour.
- » Then schedule your hour. Strive to do this one to two times/week.

- » The speaker describes a significant stress or issue in his/her life right now
- » Then switch roles
- » How did it make you feel to be listened to?
- » Did you fix anything? Did you have to fix anything?*

Continued on next page...

> **EXERCISE 11.1 CONSCIOUS LISTENING REVISITED (CONTINUED)**
>
> Thich Nhat Han recommends a full hour in each role. That may be too much, especially at first, so try 10 minutes initially and respect that boundary. Lengthen it when you are comfortable doing so.
>
> *Answer: Just being listened to can be enough. It validates you and allows you to hear your own inner wisdom.

> **EXERCISE 11.2 MINDFUL BREATHING**
>
> Mindful breathing is the practice of withdrawing your attention from distracting thoughts and redirecting your attention to your breath. By doing so, you learn to detach and become more objective, become calm and balanced, and allow yourself to be in a more connected, creative and productive space.
>
> It is normal for your mind to wander. Simply bring your attention back to your breathing, experiencing the sensation of the breath entering and leaving your body. Repeating to yourself the phrase 'I'm breathing in and out' very slowly may help.
>
> 1. In a quiet space, sit on the floor or in a chair. Sit with your back comfortably straight, hands resting on your legs. Symbolically, hands up and open means you are open to the world; hands together or down reflects inward looking.
> 2. Gently bring your attention to your breath. Don't control your breath, just observe each breath as you inhale and exhale.
> 3. Feel the cooling of your nostrils as you inhale. As you exhale, feel on your nostrils how the breath has been warmed.
>
> *Continued on next page...*

> **EXERCISE 11.2 MINDFUL BREATHING**
> **(CONTINUED)**
>
> 4. Be aware of your body as you breathe; what parts move as you breathe?
> 5. As thoughts come into your mind, acknowledge them and then gently shift your awareness back to your breathing again.
> 6. Do this for just 5 minutes each day. Increase the frequency or the amount of time as you feel drawn to. At the beginning and/or the end of your day it is a great way to start your day or prepare for sleep.
>
> Initially just observe your breathing. See if you are naturally breathing with your chest or your abdomen. Then consciously practice abdominal breathing, with your abdomen expanding as you inhale and contracting as you exhale.

> We are told that people stay in love because of chemistry or because they remain intrigued with each other, because of many kindnesses, because of luck... But part of it has got to be forgiveness and gratefulness.
>
> *Ellen Goodman*

What the Scientists are Saying

In keeping with the new positive psychology, marital scientists are now studying the positive interactions that promote intimacy and forge strong bonds. The following strategies are what successful couples use to stay happy. (Note: These are correlational studies and not intended to be a formula for success.)

- » Celebrate good news. UCLA and University of Rochester scientists found that the happiest couples were those who made the biggest deal out of good things that happen. Even small achievements, such as a deadline that was successfully met -- make a fuss over them.

- » Say nice things to each other. At the University of Washington researchers have been studying the numbers of nice vs. negative things (both verbal & non-verbal) that couples say to each another. (Laughing, touching, smiling or paying a compliment vs. eye-rolling, sneers, criticism, defensiveness, etc.). Saying "I'm sorry" after a behavior is not enough -- you need to increase the positive comments.

- » Pay attention to family and friends: It makes sense that this would place less pressure on the marriage -- relieving the relationship of full responsibility to provide for all your needs.

- » Try having sex even if you don't want to. The simple act of having sex, of giving pleasure, even if you're not in the mood, harnesses brain chemistry, unleashing the powerful bonding chemicals vasopressin and oxytocin. Experts tell low-desire couples to have sex even if they don't want to. After about five minutes of going through the motions, those bonding chemicals will release and you are likely to start enjoying yourself.

Adapted from "For Better: The Science of a Good Marriage" *Tara Parker-Pope.*

Picking A Mate

Ted Huston, a professor of human ecology at the University of Texas at Austin, has studied intimate relationships for 30 years. Huston followed 168 couples over 14 years and found that the longest and most fulfilling marriages and relationships were long friendships that unfolded with time in which the following traits emerged and grew: kindness, unconditional love for each another, and a high level of concern for others.

Daily Maintenance and Prevention Exercises

Powwows – (Exercise 3.8 and Exercise 9.1)
  Review the mantras and aspects of love by Thich Nhat Hanh at the powwows regularly.

Deep listening exercise (Exercise 3.7 and 11.1).

Go out on dates together…time alone, just the two of you, no cell phones or texting, etc.

Do fun, enjoyable, new things together---shared experiences.

> p.s. Unconditional love and support does not mean a "walk all over me, you can get your way every time" type of passivity.

You see, in life, lots of people know what to do, but few people actually do what they know. Knowing is not enough! You must take action.

Anthony Robbins

Everything you want is out there waiting for you to ask. Everything you want also wants you. But you have to take action to get it.

Jack Canfield

Section IV

Speed Bumps

OF SPECIAL NOTE......

So, what about when life happens? In this chapter I will discuss the storms of life and how to weather them and come out more than a victor (conqueror), more than just a survivor. How is it that we can face the challenges of life with grace and grow in love and renewed passion for life, becoming a thrivivor (not just a surviving, but thriving)?

Chapter 12
HOW STRESS WORKS

> Life is either a daring adventure or nothing.
> *Helen Keller*

Stress is not something we invented. I found the following statement, written by a monk nearly 2,000 years ago:

> "We trained hard—but it seemed that every time we were beginning to form up into teams, we would be reorganized. I was to learn later in life we tend to meet any new situation by reorganizing, and a wonderful method it can be for creating the illusion of progress while producing confusion, inefficiency and demoralization."
>
> *Petronius Arbiter (Satyricon, 66 A.D.)*

Stress crosses all boundaries, regardless of level of civilization, sophistication, intelligence or walk of life. Stress makes for a short trip to depression and disease (dis-ease).

Stressors:

» Health issues: mental illness, chronic disease, life-threatening conditions, drug or alcohol abuse, chronic pain, depression.

» Work: downsizing, retooling, unrealistic expectations, bullying, politics.

» Personal challenges: change, fear, depression, single status, living alone, family challenges because of human growth and family stage changes.

» Maturational changes: personal growth stages, midlife crisis, empty nest. (Just a note….contrary to everything you have heard, all alternatives to aging are baaaaaaad.)

Bless this stress? C. Leslie Charles and Mimi Donaldson, in their book *Bless Your Stress*, say a resounding YES! All the new research into the physics of human energy supports this. Energy attracts like energy, so if you bless your stress, blessings will come your way. If you whine and complain, you will get more of the same. "If you keep doing what you've always done, you'll keep getting what you've always had." Mark Twain said it. Buddha said it. Jesus did not tell us to pray saying, "Hallowed be thy name….if you send me blessings." He said, bless Him anyway.

We are just beginning to understand stress and its effects on the body. And we are just beginning to understand it at the cellular level in the brain. NIMH (the National Institute for Mental Health) published a study by Jing Du, M.D., Ph.D., and Husseini Manji, M.D., in a Science Update in February 2009. Their study showed that the fight-or-flight hormones (glucocorticoids) provide extra energy for brain cells to adapt to acute challenges, allowing a person to act quickly in an emergency. Chronic stress and, hence, chronic elevation of glucocorticoid levels may reduce cell function (fatigue) and "may be at the root of certain physical and mental illnesses."

In other words, some stress is not all bad. It stimulates the body for action and indirectly, survival…fight or flight. But the problem comes with chronic stress, when we are not able to use up the stress hormones through fight or flight, that energy turns inward, causing disease.

Stress is what happens to our body when we experience a threat, whether real or imagined. Hans Selye wrote the first book on stress (*The Stress of Life*). He developed a model for stress called the general adaptation syndrome (GAS), or stress syndrome, in which the body experiences three distinct phases:

1) Alarm reaction.
2) Resistance.
3) Exhaustion.

The alarm phase, also known as the fight-or-flight response, is the body's reaction to acute stress, which leaves our mouths with that awful aftertaste from the adrenaline rush. Our bodies are actually hardwired to this response. Resistance is the next phase. With prolonged stress, we find ways to cope and adapt. In the last phase, the body's resources are eventually depleted the body is unable to maintain normal function (homeostasis) and long-term damage ensues, resulting in disease such as colds, flus, heart disease, hypertension and cancer. It is valuable to note that even too much good stress – eustress -- can lead to disruption of homeostasis and distress.

Quantum theory – the idea that everything is energy -- is especially fascinating when applied to the human body. The fight-or-flight response releases a cocktail of hormones designed for maximal energy use (to fight or to run). This reaction is no longer adaptive, and the energy, when it is not used up, turns inward. Channeling this energy, finding appropriate outlets to release it can come in the form of journaling, exercise, positive thinking, etc. The key is having a variety of these strategies ready and finding which one(s) work best for you in various situations.

New research demonstrates a new dimension of the stress reaction: the "tend and befriend" behavior. Women, more often than men, when faced with a threat or stressed, will become protective or will seek out social support. Given women's historic and traditional role of childcare, this behavior makes sense. It was a survival strategy for themselves and their children that has become hard-wired.

Additional notes:

- » On a spiritual level, stress is the perceived separation from our divine source, which is an illusion but nonetheless causes fear.
- » A common theme to stress is loss.
- » Though stress is inevitable, it can be managed.
- » Anger and fear are the stress emotions (for fight and flight, respectively).

> "It's not what happens to us, but our reaction…that causes us stress…. Most important decision we can make each day is our choice of attitude…. It is the way I choose to see the world that will create the world I see."

(Joan Lunden, in *Stressed is Desserts Spelled Backwards*)

It is also important to recognize that the threats we have today are not physical but mental, emotional or spiritual, with perhaps 90 percent of perceived threats being of a spiritual nature, involving relationships, values and purpose in life (Henry Grayson).

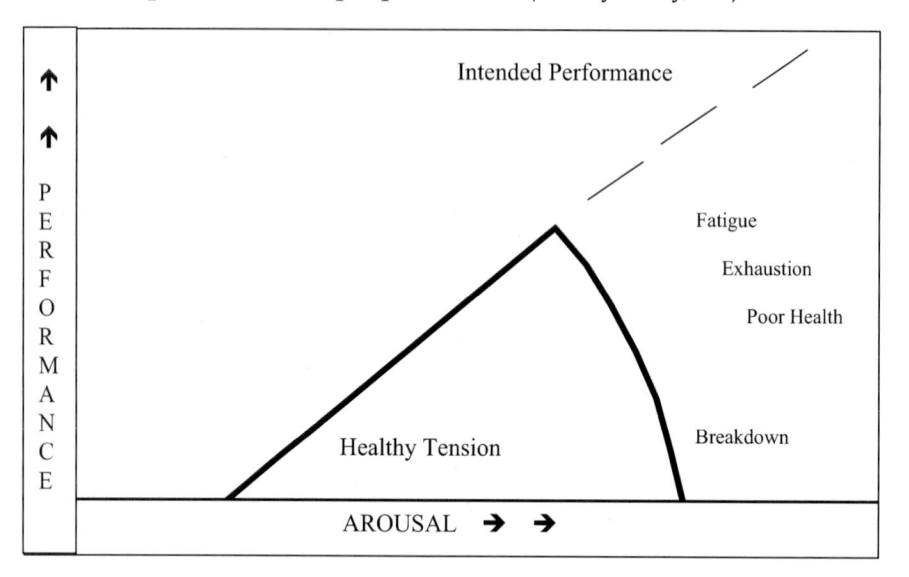

PERFORMANCE (vertical axis) vs *AROUSAL* (horizontal axis): a curve rising from "Healthy Tension" to a peak, then falling through "Fatigue", "Exhaustion", "Poor Health", to "Breakdown"; a dashed line labeled "Intended Performance" continues upward.

The above diagram is a classic for describing the relationship between stress and performance. At some point, the stress is too much, resulting in fatigue, exhaustion and disease.

I recently received one of those anonymous e-mails that had this gem to say:

> A lecturer when explaining stress management to an audience raised a glass of water and asked "How heavy is this glass of water?" Answers called out ranged from 20g to 500g. The lecturer replied, "The absolute weight doesn't matter. It depends on how long you try to hold it.
>
> "If I hold it for a minute, that's not a problem.
> "If I hold it for an hour, I'll have an ache in my right arm.
> "If I hold it for a day, you'll have to call an ambulance.
>
> "In each case, it's the same weight, but the longer I hold it, the heavier it becomes.

"And that's the way it is with stress management. If we carry our burdens all the time, sooner or later, as the burden becomes increasingly heavy, we won't be able to carry on.

"As with the glass of water, you have to put it down for a while and rest before holding it again. When we're refreshed, we can carry on with the burden.

"So, before you return home tonight, put the burden of work down. Don't carry it home. You can pick it up tomorrow.

"Whatever burdens you're carrying now, set them down for a moment if you can."

So my friend, put down anything that may be a burden to you right now. Don't pick it up again until after you've rested a while.

Chapter 13
A WORD ABOUT FEAR

> I am an old man and *have* known a great many troubles, but *most* of them *never happened*.
>
> Albert Einstein

Free-falling

Imagine that you are free-falling through time and space... infinite space above and below you. No cares, no worries, just the air in your hair, bolstered up by nothing but the breeze and the blue sky all around you. Life seems to be going all your way, then **ZZZZJNG!** Life throws you a curve ball. Do you take it full force, letting it spin you out of control? Can you truly take the guide cords of your own life? Change the course of your life? At this point in time it doesn't feel as if you can. You might know you can handle anything, that you'll never be given more than you can handle, but here and now, you're life has just been rocked. You can consciously decide to rebuild, to let go, to move on, to live. Healing takes time, but we have been created with an unbelievable ability to heal ourselves. All we need to do is tap into it.

Now, that curve ball. Was it the death of a loved one, the loss of a job or fear? Fear that shakes you to your very fiber...with possible outcomes that can make or break you and those you love. How can you survive? How can you get through it with peace and calm? And then, how can you do better than that and live again...at peace with yourself and others?

Fear. They say that animals can smell it. That day when my husband and I hit a patch of black ice and the world suddenly slowed down, and as we spun around and gracefully slid off the freeway... everything was in slow motion. I can even remember looking straight into the eyes of the driver and passenger in the car behind us. In reality, there was not even the time but to do anything but say "Oh please," straight from the heart. Immediately afterwards I could taste that bitter taste of the adrenaline rush and sat shaking with reaction.

Fear. Then there is that gut-wrenching, mind-numbing fear. Imagine having your only child, young still, at age 21, being given counterfeited money orders for a room she was subletting. You know to your very fiber that she is innocent...you were there for every step of the process...and now, to face every morning the reality that if justice doesn't prevail, she may end up in jail...that her hopes for being a teacher are gone forever...that she said to me, "I can't be separated from my family, life wouldn't be worth living," her "life would be ended". Her freedom threatened. The new buds of her fragile independence shattered even as she started poking her head out into the world. What would my life be like with her in jail? How can I go on as usual? My child. Her pain is mine.

It was interesting watching myself. It was as if a disembodied consciousness was observing this person go through the motions of life.

I have been in tough places before. I was a single mom: one year after I bought a new-to-me house, I'm laid off, and then two years later, I'm laid off again. I set up my own businesses at that time and income was a month-to-month thing for many years. I've faced down cancer. I've had grief: my mother died, and I lost my home, job and husband through divorce, all in the space of a couple of years, but nothing was like this. Shattering. Immobilizing. My child, my heart.

The following is something I wrote as I was experiencing it:

> How is it that I am keeping my balance? How is it that I am continuing to breathe, in and out? How is it that I am continuing to put one foot in front of the other? Not only that, but I'm still creative as I teach; light bulbs are going off for me and my students. In a simple CPR class, several students asked for my business card, evaluations remarking on "a great & interesting class," "I will be well prepared."
>
> Why did I wake up Friday morning with such a feeling of peace?

In the face of catastrophic events, how do you cope? How do you keep up the façade and keep going in to work everyday? How can you maintain any peace of mind?

Sleep certainly helps. Continuing to eat right, drink plenty of fluids, take my vitamins and medicines is a very good thing. Staying connected helps too. My daughter and I are certainly sharp with each other at times, but we immediately identified it and apologized.

But that doesn't account for all of it. My body is staying outwardly healthy...no colds or flus. I have horrible chest pain from indigestion; my guts are belying the peace of my mind, as are the sporadic tears and fatigue. It's that good-ol' fight-or-flight mechanism that was hard-wired into our bodies thousands upon thousands of years ago, and it is working overtime. I wish I could say that my yoga, meditation and prayer are able to control even these hard-wired symptoms, but I am just your average Joe. I am still striving for that (absolute peace in the storm of life), still wrestling with those old superstitions of "knock on wood," and "don't say it because it tempts fate."

I feel totally disembodied, as if I'm watching a play and I know what the characters are thinking, I can feel their tears but still, I am calm because I know that it will work out for the better (whatever form that may be), and yet...the uncertainty of the outcome...try as I might, I can't dissociate myself from the outcome. I just want this to be over. I can know up the wazoo that there are others facing worse...that the people of Iran are daily living with the unbearable stress of war in Iran, Ruwandan genocide, the tsunami of 2006, the Pakastani earthquakes and landslides. Our situation is miniscule and has a finite time frame by comparison. While sobering, this doesn't seem to restore me to my previous level of LIFE.

Stress is a curious thing…such a letdown after a flurry of activity, where I was fighting with words, wrestling with concepts and clarity to make the clearest case/best case for the lawyer. The let-down feeling after all that intense activity. Now, with all that pent-up energy from fight-or-flight, I just want to pick a fight with someone. My disembodied self sees this and I've taken action -- or rather, inaction. I don't want to put myself in a situation where I might say something I'll regret, something I don't mean, so I am deliberately staying away from my friend.

> **Courage is not the absence of fear.**
> **Courage is what you do despite it.**

How was it that I was able to stay sane and at peace most of the time? According to the dictionary, hope and courage are the opposite of fear. But I had heard once, and find it to be true, that courage is not the absence of fear -- courage is what you do despite fear. Because, beyond a doubt, the fear was called for. This was a very real threat to my daughter. Fear activates the fight-or-flight mechanism that has been hard-wired in us since the beginning of time when we were chased by sabertooth tigers. When faced with a threat, we don't want to be immobilized by fear (those who were, were at a *slight* evolutionary disadvantage 30,000 years ago), we want to act now. Sometimes that means stand and fight; sometimes that means *run*. And here, for me, at this time, that meant wrestling with words to create the clearest document, going to work and school every day, doing yoga, providing a strong, confident support to my daughter so that she could continue to go to work and school, with a modicum of peace and calm.

Seeking sanctuary. This is not a place where I found all the answers, but a place where I could calm my mind and breathe, and breathe again, and again, where I could "Be still and know" (Proverbs 17:22a) that in my heart of hearts, everything would be OK.

Sanctuary is a place where what I call *mud mind* or *stinkin' thinkin'* slows down so there are spaces between my thoughts. A place where you can contemplate...

> That which cannot be seen is called invisible.
> That which cannot be heard is called inaudible.
> That which cannot be held is called intangible...
>
> By intuition you can see it,
> Hear it,
> And feel it.
>
> Approach it and there is no beginning;
> follow it and there is no end.
> You cannot know it, but you can be it,
> at ease in your own life.
>
> Discovering how things have always been brings one into harmony
> with the Way
> [...and brings peace]
>
> *Tao Te Ching, 14th verse*

So, when faced with a world-shattering curve ball in your life, take it like a speed bump, as our lawyer said. Get plenty of sleep, keep eating right, drink plenty of fluids, take your vitamins and medicines, and stay connected. And to help you maintain your peace of mind, seek out your sanctuary. Set it up now, so that you will be in practice, with a toned heart and mind, peaceful and tranquil, ready to face stress.

EXERCISE 13.1   CREATING A SANCTUARY REVISITED

A place where your eyes see that:

> Every tree and plant in the meadow seemed to be dancing,
> those which average eyes would see as fixed and still.
>
> *Rumi*

- » Eliminate as many distractions as you can.
- » Create triggers for yourself: aromatic oils, incense or visual triggers that make the space special.
- » Avoid using your bed or sitting at your desk.

Continued on next page...

> **EXERCISE 13.1 CREATING A SANCTUARY REVISITED (CONTINUED)**
>
> » Prepare yourself ahead: take a bath, a walk, eat or drink consciously, practice some yoga or tai chi.
> » Sit properly and with good posture.
>
> You may be able to make use of a time when no one is in the office…make it different from just sitting at your desk, though -- make it special.
>
> With practice, these triggers can induce relaxation.
> With practice, you can meditate anywhere.
> With practice, you will see the trees dancing.
>
> (See also Exercise 4.1)

Below is a decision tree to guide you in coping with sadness and depression.

Depression Decision Tree

Are any of the following present? o Slowed thought and decision-making process o Excessive crying, indigestion o Preoccupation with death o Thoughts of suicide	Yes	Tell someone who can help immediately. Consult a crisis hot line or physician by telephone now
No		

Have any of the following been present longer than a week? ○ Irritability, restlessness ○ Loss of interest in activities or hobbies once pleasurable, including sex ○ Fatigue and decreased energy ○ Difficulty concentrating, remembering details and making decisions ○ Insomnia, early-morning wakefulness or excessive sleeping ○ Overeating or appetite loss ○ Persistent aches or pains, headaches, cramps or digestive problems that do not ease even with treatment People with depressive illnesses do not all experience the same symptoms. The severity, frequency and duration of symptoms will vary depending on the individual and his or her particular illness. (Courtesy of: NIMH)	**Yes**	Apply Home Treatment **AND** Make an appointment with a counselor today

No		

Apply Home Treatment: See Stress Relief Flow Chart	Yes	And
		  o Make a plan
		  o Set boundaries (when you will have the phone on, whom will you answer it for)
		  o Consider a land line for general use, cell phone for limited use: emergencies and select individuals/times.

Stress Relief Flow Chart

Create a Sanctuary (See Ex. 4.1 and 13.1)

Space, time, quiet, meditate, breathe

Simplify Your Life

Simplify your schedule, workspace, living space
Limit use of cell phones and technology,
Practice enoughness (see Chapter 6).

Practice Self-Care

Eat, sleep, fluids, vitamins, zinc, exercise, yoga and tai chi.

Make a plan: simplify, money management, time management, volunteer, have meaningful social interactions.

Maybe most important: schedule play time,
relaxing time, doing nothing time.

One evening, in January 2010, while vegging in front of the television, my daughter turned to me and asked, "Am I making these things happen to myself or am I just a victim of circumstance? Is there something wrong with me?" My response was to have her reflect...if the outcome was unpleasant, are there parts of her own behavior that she could change in the future to change the outcome? Specifically, in the situations in which she found herself the past two years, she could ask, "Am I over-reacting? Am I being too harsh?" Additionally, the stress load she is under...that is inherent with her age: being in college and experiencing unavoidable life events (two grandfathers' illnesses and subsequent deaths, facing jail if justice does not prevail) make it so that little things can tip the scales.

So, when life happens, or to be best prepared when it does happen, remember:

- Human nature is such that, for whatever reason, misery is easier. Happiness is work. You decide.
- Everything is energy...we are participating in creation.
- "If you continue in the same direction, you're likely to end up where you are headed" (Tao Te Ching).
- Decrease your overall stress load (make a sanctuary for yourself; simplify your life; manage your time, money, exercise, and nutrition, and sleep well; laugh and play; have meaningful social interactions [volunteer if you have no other outlet for this].
- Reflect on the issues, learn from them, and if you don't like it, get yourself unstuck and change it. Don't just sit there and lick your wounds.
- Choose happiness. Choose what you think about (Ex. 3.2 - 3.5).
- Seek social support. We need it to be resilient, it's part of the denominator, we *are* social beings.
- With this attitude, if we truly can't change the situation, we adapt, we find a way to live with it, and in some instances, research has shown that we can even learn to like it.

All emotions stem from either love or fear. So if whatever is going on is not of love, then it is of fear. Fear of the unknown is perhaps one of the worst things to cope with, so it makes sense to face your fear. Ask yourself, "What is it I am afraid of here?" Then, "What's the worst that can happen?" (That one really valuable piece of wisdom that my mother gave me.) Now you can strategize. If that's the worst that can happen, you can be prepared. Anything less is frosting. You are now empowered.

> "The future belongs to those who believe in the beauty of their dreams."
>
> *Eleanor Roosevelt*
>
> NOTE: Keep your eye on your dream.

Need more convincing that there is power in positive thought?

David McClelland, a behavioral psychologist at Harvard, performed a series of studies in the 1980s called "The Mother Teresa Effect." While viewing videos of Mother Teresa working compassionately among India's poor, his Harvard students experienced increased Immunoglobin-A (IgA) (your first line of defense against colds and flus). The next phase of the research tested the simple act of imagining the love they felt for someone. Both exercises had the same effects on the immune system.

So if we focus on love and compassion, gratefulness and blessings, this makes us healthier, creating more blessings. If we stress ourselves out, we tend to get sick. See how that works? We get more of the same. We create our own reality.

> **EXERCISE 13.2   COUNT YOUR BLESSINGS**
>
> »   On a notecard, make a list of your blessings and put it in a prominent place.
> »   Start a blessing journal or a combined joy and blessings journal. Write in it every day.

What we really would like to be able to do is to stay calm and keep a clear mind in the midst of the storms around us. To have mental and emotional resilience so that even when rocked, we bend, but we will not break. "Emotional well-being is the ability to feel and express the full range of human emotions and to control them, not be controlled by them" (Brian Luke Seaward). It is to have the freedom to act rather than react.

Just as we have been told to take care of our hair, our teeth, our nutritional health, we need to take care of our minds. Relax, we've been told. Take a break. Has it worked? Sometimes; not always. The truth is, the traditional ways we have of relaxing, of taking a brain break, changing activities, slowing down...our minds are still processing. We need tools to control the traffic. "Meditation is about keeping the mind strong, clear, and resilient" [*Mental Resilience*] (See meditation ex. 4.2 - 4.6).

SPEED BUMPS...
With Practice, You Will See the Trees Dancing

> "When going through hell, keep going."
> *Winston Churchill*

There are times in our lives when in the scheme of things and in the interests of the ultimate fulfillment of our goals and happiness, self-care takes a back seat while we get work done. Whether it's the classes to get to complete our degree (on top of managing job and kids) or care of an aging/ill parent, sometimes we are worked off our feet, exhausted and with literally no time for ourselves, be it for exercise or sanctuary. Take a reality check. As soon as you realize what is happening, regroup. Do you need to reprioritize for the short or long term? Remember, if you don't take care of yourself, what you do give to your school work or parent may be greatly reduced in quality.

The following two verses tell us to stay rooted, be calm, be master of ourselves.

> The heavy is the root of the lights.
> The still is the master of unrest.
>
> Realizing this,
> The successful person is poised and centered
> In the midst of all activities;
> Although surrounded by opulence,
> he is not swayed.
>
> Why should the lord of the country
> Flit about like a fool?
> If you let yourself be blown to and fro,
> You lose touch with your root.
> To be restless is to lose one's self-mastery.
>
> *Tao Te Ching, 26th verse*

Be still and know that I am God.

(Psalm 46:10)

EXERCISE 13.3 CHOOSE YOUR ATTITUDE
JOURNAL TOPIC

We have the power to control our level of stress and even to choose not to react to it at all.

Yesterday. I'm driving out of a parking lot after an antiques show, there was a man standing on the corner, with his hand way up, giving me the finger. He caught my eye and started nodding vigorously. And he started mouthing the two words at me repeatedly. What kind of day was he having? What was his choice of attitudes as he got out of bed that morning? He has my undying compassion.

What is your attitude when you get up in the morning? What can you do to choose your attitude? Will you choose an attitude of gratitude or let stress get you down?

EXERCISE 13.4 CHOOSE YOUR ACTION
JOURNAL TOPIC – CHOOSE TO ACT, NOT REACT

Many people have been victimized or treated badly, whether by bullying, sibling rivalry or harsh words from a parent. Even if the incident was minor, the effects can remain with us for a long time. When was the last time you were the target of such behavior? What could you do differently to change your reaction or change the whole dynamics of the situation?

Chapter 14
EXPECTATIONS

Do you think you can take over the universe and improve it?
I do not believe it can be done.

Everything under heaven is a sacred vessel and cannot be controlled.
Trying to control leads to ruin.
Trying to grasp, we lose.
Allow your life to unfold naturally.
Know that it too is a vessel of perfection.
Just as you breathe in and breathe out
There is a time for being ahead
And a time for being behind;
A time for being in motion
And a time for being at rest;
At time for being vigorous
And a time for being exhausted;
A time for being safe
And a time for being in danger.

Tao Te Ching, v. 29

"He hath made everything beautiful in his time."

Ecclesiastes, 3:11a, KJV

Much growth is stunted by too careful prodding,
Too eager tenderness.
The things we love we have to learn to leave alone.

"Woman with Flower," Poem by Naomi Long Madgett

- » When you find yourself angry, look for an unmet expectation.
- » Expectations can lead to frustration and anger.
- » Stop judging others.
- » Accept things you can't change.
- » There are some healthy expectations in relationships. Find

them, negotiate them. Personal safety, communication and a healthy, growing relationship are some of the basics.

The Serenity Prayer

God grant me the serenity
to accept the things I cannot change;
courage to change the things I can;
and wisdom to know the difference.

-Reinhold Niebuhr

EXERCISE 14.1   EXPECTATIONS JOURNAL

A. Make a concise list of your key stressors (people or situations), such as work, boss, children, elder-care, finances.

_____

_____

_____

_____

Continued on next page...

Exercise 14.1   Expectations Journal (continued)

B. Pick one from above. _____ What are your expectations of that person or situation?

_____

_____

_____

_____

C. What do you expect to give in this relationship? Examples: money, guidance, cooking, cleaning, house maintenance, child-rearing practices, vacations, together/separate, alone time

_____

_____

_____

_____

D. Now, look at each these expectations in B above, and ask yourself:

    Is it reasonable?
    Can you do this for yourself?
    Should you do this for yourself?
    Have you clearly communicated it?
    Is there another way to achieve it?
    Do you need to renegotiate?

> **EXERCISE 14.2 ITS TIME WILL COME**
>
> Practice recognizing that there's a time for everything
>
> Stifle your inclination to interfere.
>
> List an issue at home or work that is bugging you, that just doesn't seem to be going right.
>
> _____
> _____
> _____
> _____
>
> Make a decision to observe it peacefully. See how things turn out when left alone. Consider journaling on it several times/week or even daily. When it seems peaceful and natural for you to provide your 2 cents' worth, do so.

Barriers

Barriers are things in our lives that we allow to limit our capacity to reach the goals we desire, things that can prevent us from being happy and joyful. They can be as physical as a handicap, or emotional and behavioral barriers. Whichever they are, they limit function...if you let them.

I despise heights. You could even say that I am afraid of heights, and you would be correct. Along with the rest of the world, I used to call it dysfunctional and even neurotic. Then I came to understand the condition. It is important to note that fear was designed to be a life-saving reaction. I have what is called height vertigo. This is a depth perception phenomenon that makes me dizzy when I am up high and see several objects at vastly differing heights, such as from a bridge or the top of a lighthouse. If you're up high and dizzy, what can happen? You can fall. The trip off the top of the Eiffel Tower is not a pleasant one, I understand. So a fear of heights, given my height vertigo, is actually healthy.

But my fear of heights can be a very handicapping barrier. I once was assigned a corner office on the seventh floor, complete with ceiling-to-floor windows. I also like adventure and traveling, so crossing bridges and climbing lighthouses or the Eiffel Tower could be problematic…if I let it.

> It is said that courage is not the absence of fear,
> courage is what you do despite it.

So…I accommodate. I find a way to do it anyway. I go up the stairs of lighthouses on my behind, looking at the wall until I get to the top. I drive on the inner lane of a bridge, turning off all distractions, do my yoga breathing and sally forth. At work, as I went around the modular walls next to the window, I faced the modular wall. My chair was at the back of the cubical, with the desk in between me and the window. Determination. Focus. Values. And in the words of my British ancestors, sheer cussedness.

Emotional and behavioral handicaps can be more difficult to conceptualize. They are learned communication and behavior patterns -- things you saw or learned to do that felt comfortable at one level but no longer have any adaptive or functional use and can impair your happiness. In other words, they are now dysfunctional.

So, if you find that you are experiencing dissonance, angst, a seeming inability to succeed at what you want to do, look for the root. Then, let it go. If you can't find the root, seek out a better pattern of interaction. The book *Mindful Loving*, Grayson, provides workable methods for helping to erase negative core beliefs that lead to dysfunctional behavior patterns.

> Remember, Edison developed at least 3,000
> light bulbs before he got one to work.

You are not your fear or handicap unless you believe it is so -- because then your belief makes it so. Your actions and reactions are guided by this belief and reinforce it. You are their creator.

The following two exercises can walk you through the steps needed for you to analyze your barriers and work through solutions to find what works for you.

EXERCISE 14.3 VALUES, BARRIERS AND STRENGTHS JOURNAL TOPIC

First
- » Title one of the pages VALUES.
- » List your values.

Next:
- » Title one of your journal pages BARRIERS.
- » List as many as you can, leaving space to add more later.
- » Then highlight the two to three that you would like to work on. Consider the most problematic, or what will make the biggest impact, which is the easiest to accomplish (thereby giving you a feeling of success) or a combination of these.

Then:
- » Give your next page the title STRENGTHS.
- » List as many strengths as you can, leave space to add more later.
- » NOTE: Often our strengths are reflections of our handicaps. (ex: Independent: can't accept help)

> **EXERCISE 14.4   JOURNAL TOPIC:**
> **WHAT AREAS DO I NEED TO CONCENTRATE ON TO GET WHERE I WANT TO GO?**
>
> Draw the following table in your journal, then start filling it in
>
> | Areas needing work | Barriers (reasons not to change, things that support and reinforce this behavior) | Pros/cons to giving up this behavior | Pros/cons to keeping this behavior |
> |---|---|---|---|
> | | | | |
> | | | | |
>
> Draw the following table in your journal and start filling in each column.
>
> | Area needing work | Rank (High, medium, low) | Options/Solutions/ Strategies | Pros/Cons of Options | Rank Options |
> |---|---|---|---|---|
> | | | | | |
> | | | | | |
> | | | | | |

Change

- » Whenever we can't change our circumstances, we adapt.
- » If the way you are dealing with your situation works for you, good. If not, change it. Don't stay stuck

> Let your heart be at peace.
> Amidst the rush of worldly comings and goings,
> Observe how endings become beginnings.
>
> *Tao Te Ching, v.16*

Change happens. "Change is inevitable, and with change comes fear, particularly fear of the unknown" (*Quiet Mind, Fearless Heart*, Brian Luke Seaward). Change is stress, for good or bad, positive or negative.

Change happens. It is either imposed from outside or chosen. When it is chosen: We are frequently making changes in our lives -- redecoration, new job, new house. More, more, more, better and better. Do we ever stop to ask why? Will it make us happier? Will its costs outweigh its benefits? E.g., do we really need the angst of a car payment, or with a little work, will the old car/no payment give us the reliable transportation we need?

When it is imposed on us: Sometimes we just need to say, "I'll get through this."

Many changes are what we call maturational changes. Such as those that take place between 18 and 24 years of age: leaving school; getting a job; assuming responsibility; experiencing the urge to merge. Though you're excited about the future and things you've planned for, you are in some sense leaving behind a routine, a life that you have built: school (19 to 20 years of your life has been spent in school), connections with friends, parents. All of these relationships are being renegotiated... all at once. (See Erickson's Stages of Psychosocial Development and maturational milestones.)

In physics, stress is the force or pressure applied to an object, enough to bend or break it. We would do well to learn from the palm tree, which bends in the face of 200 mph winds and does not break. On a spiritual level, stress is the absence of inner peace. An ancient Chinese proverb says that tension is who you think you should be. Relaxation is who you are. So learn to relax and bend with the force of the wind.

Be here now

> Worrying about what is past is like crying over spilt milk.
>
> Worrying about the future is to worry about things that may never happen and probably never will
>
> Both activities use up the precious present.

You get to decide how to spend that precious time. This doesn't mean that you don't think about the future. When met with challenges, we must give thought to how to meet them gracefully. Contingency planning is necessary. Taking the opportunity to regroup and see if you are being pointed in a new direction, what is it you are meant to learn from this. Then trust. Trust that the Source who has given you life will support you through these changes and into a space that is whole.

Other famous trueisms:
> What will be, will be.
> Don't sweat the small stuff.
> This, too, shall pass.
> So, enjoy the here and now.

> Sometimes we need to keep our eye on the goal (joy, happiness, financial security).

If you look off into the distance at your goal, you will be able to traverse the straightest line possible, rather than stumbling over the path on your way. Always note the irony here: be in the now but keep your eye on the goal. It is a balancing act. When the waters are rough, you have to keep breathing through it, but your focus may be more on the goal even while you're remembering to enjoy the journey as much as possible.

Strong Emotional Reactions

A strong emotional reaction to something -- anger, humiliation, etc. -- is a signal that something needs your attention. Often this is not due to what we initially think of as the "triggering event." Despite its discomfort, awareness and exploration of this triggering event is an opportunity for healing, a time for introspection and discovery. Chances are, the upset is due to an ego misinterpretation, an old way of operation. So take a breath and just be a witness. Then, from the perspective of cool detachment, decide what your action will be.

What is action? What is inaction?
- » Both Martin Luther King, Jr., and Ghandi stood for the positive force of inaction.
- » Buddha: "One who sees inaction in action, and action in inaction, is intelligent among men, and he is in the transcendental position, although engaged in all sorts of activities" (Chapter IV: v. 18 Bhagavad-Gita).

HOME TREATMENT – Strong Emotional Reactions

When an emotion stops serving our well-being, we need to develop an understanding of how to drop it. The following exercise can help you do that.

EXERCISE 14.5   TIE ONE ON

Triggering event – describe it: I broke the turn signal lever on my mother's car.

Internal reaction – explain your reaction: the judgments and evaluations that are going on in your head. Stop and consciously sort through your thoughts and feelings on this issue. Decide on their validity. Is this true or untrue? Does this reaction have any value to you today? Pull out and use that tool my mother gave me and ask, "What's the worst that can happen?" I was a basket case when I broke my mother's car. But sanity finally returned. Well, it was an accident. It's broken. I'll just get it fixed. So I went in and told my parents that I would get it fixed. Sanity. It was a $100 fix.

External response – describe it: your behavior, what you say or do. Begin to observe what sets you off.

Adapted from Bless Your Stress by C. Leslie Charles and Mimi Donaldson

Now, make a decision -- act rather than react. Choose your action. In this case, I went in and said I'd get an estimate and get it fixed. Practice acting, rather than reacting.

Worry and Fear

> Fear is at the root of anything not love

Fear
- » Learn to see the problems in your life as gifts.
- » Stop worrying.
- » Tackle the things you fear...exercise the courage muscle.
- » Choose love instead of fear.

Henry Grayson, in his book *Mindful Loving* says that all emotions can be distilled down to two basic ones: love and fear. And that all positive emotions -- joy, happiness, delight and affection -- grow out of love. Similarly, all negative emotions -- anger, jealousy, guilt, envy, hurt, rage -- grow out of fear. The more intense or pervasive the negative emotion, the greater is the fear that gives rise to it. The stress reaction is fear.

He also contends that we all have one basic negative core belief: that we are separate instead of interconnected with all others, the universe or God. There is also the basic trauma of unlovableness that underlies all the others.

> **A New Perspective:**
>
> See other people's reactions as an appeal for love instead of the attack or rejection that it appears to be.

By making such a perceptual shift change, creating this new reality, we no longer perceive an attack and can feel compassion, not fear or anger. By doing so, we are less likely to invite retaliation or defensiveness. We begin to erase that original negative core belief.

"Fear...seems to work like a magnetic force field, often attracting that which is feared into one's life"......(Grayson). Do you remember in "Ghostbusters" the river of slime running under the city and how it took on the emotions of those around it? Anger and hatred brought it to a boil; music calmed it. The analogies in this are astounding.

Negative emotions, just like pain, are signals that something is wrong. When we feel pain, we try to pinpoint where, when, what affects it. When our emotions come into play, we often take the first available explanation and react. When we take the time to examine the emotion, though, it is often not what we think it is. It is often the product of the "Sure Enough" principle, an erroneous thought system (ego thinking) that serves to justify and support our beliefs about ourselves, beliefs that we are separate, that we are victims. For example: Just a few months after my Dad died, my dear friend and mentor, Alice, died. All I wanted was peace and normalcy. The college had cut one of my three contracts for the spring. My immediate reaction: "This gal is out to get me;" "I can't live on this." I had a definite edge to my voice, shrill with emotion. Now, however, I know that it was one of the best things that ever happened. It gave me the opportunity to write this book. I had defined peace as sameness. No one was out to get me. The administrator was just operating out of what she thought was best for the college. Granted, she understood that she was cutting my hours, but that was incidental to the purpose. My reaction was a flag that I, not surprisingly, was still grieving and healing.

Still in the name of self-protection, and self-preservation, the "ego wants us to question our inherent self-worth, or loveableness, our essential goodness (i.e., creates fear). It wants us to question and doubt our commitments to the people we love, it wants to undermine our trust in our fellow human beings, including ourselves" (Grayson).

Recognizing ego's voice is the first step. A conscious decision not to listen to its false advice is the next. We can choose thoughts of fear -- and with it, anxiety, anger, pain, hatred and the sure-enough principle -- or thoughts of love -- and along with it, peace, joy and happiness.

Remember: All emotions not based on love are fear-based. For practical purposes, the opposite of love is not hate but fear.

Perspectives on Unemployment, Underemployment or Job Dissatisfaction

When our jobs are not satisfying, one option is to regroup and move on. When this is simply not feasible, it helps to seek other ways in our lives to make contributions. If we are providing for our families, what's not satisfying about that? Generally this issue speaks to where we are in life. According to Erik Ericson, the developmental task of middle adulthood (ages 35 to 55 or 65) is Generativity vs. Self-absorption or Stagnation. Here is the source of that black cloud called midlife crisis. So, if we are not finding an inherent source of satisfaction that we are contributing to the big picture in our lifework, we get this feeling of dissatisfaction. Having recognized this need for generativity as the source of our dissatisfaction, we can get to work and find other avenues by which to fulfill our lives.

Spend time reflecting on this. Come to an understanding and seek to fill the void. See the section on maturational changes and Ericson's developmental stages in the table below for further insights.

Don't Just Fill the Void

When dissatisfied, don't just fill a void or find the easiest target -- take time to find the true source of the issue.

This is the story of George and Sylvia. Both are 46, married for 25 years with no children. Sylvia is a stay-at-home housewife with a jewelry-making business that pays for itself but nothing else. George has a great paying, but unsatisfying job. George's reflections to a friend were: "If only she would get a job we could save up and I could retire early with enough money to cover the health costs. Then I could pursue a hobby, too."

George ended up jettisoning Sylvia and immediately filling the void with a girlfriend who had a whole new set of problems (alcohol abuse, poor earnings, single mom). Or are they just the same dependency issues packaged differently -- something to shake up the status quo in the illusion of making it better?

Maturational Changes

We are questors. We are on a journey. Abraham Maslow's Hierarchy of Human Needs illustrates the various stages (see Appendix 2). The concept is that, once the most basic needs are met, we are then free to satisfy personal growth needs. Because we are questors, even when we like our jobs, our homes, our families, a niggling feeling of discontent and unrest can creep in. It's that old friend Ego come to visit, saying, "There must be something else"; "How long can this last?" And according to the "Sure Enough" principle, this feeling of discontent is energy that begins to communicate itself subtly to those around you, and what was thought now becomes reality.

Again, what that niggling feeling is is the natural human need for personal growth. The highest level is purpose and fulfillment -- being everything you can be.

Solution? Observe it from the perspective of a clear mind and with detachment. Is change really called for? If not, recognize that this may just be human nature, and don't let it take control rashly. Recognize the power of thought and take control of it, rather than let it control your happiness and contentment.

See the developmental stages below. The last three can be especially useful to understanding some of the issues and concerns inherent at each stage.

Erickson's Stages of Psychosocial Development

Hope: Trust vs. Mistrust (infants, birth to 1 year)

Will: Autonomy vs. Shame and Doubt (toddlers, 2 to 3 years)

Purpose: Initiative vs. Guilt (preschool, 4 to 6 years)

Competence: Industry vs. Inferiority (childhood, 7 to 12 years)

Fidelity: Identity vs. Role Confusion (adolescents, 13 to 19 years)

Love: Intimacy vs. Isolation (young adults, 20 to 34 years)

Care: Generativity vs. Stagnation (middle adulthood, 35 to 65 years)

Wisdom: Ego Integrity vs. Despair (seniors, 65 years onwards)

Illness and Pain

Acute Illness

I am experiencing the adventures of empty nest for a second time. A year after my daughter got married and move 2,200 miles away, I took on two teen-aged foreign exchange students. As I write this they are gone now just 1½ months. Two days after they left, I came down with a cold that took me out of commission for almost three weeks. It took me an additional three weeks since my outward physical recovery and return of energy for my frame of mind to adjust itself. I was fairly concerned over my apathy toward anything that wasn't "filling the void." I have watched more TV in the past six weeks than in the past 12 months. I firmly believe that the illness was a huge part of that picture. I consciously had to keep telling myself to breathe, it would get better; interest, energy and enthusiasm for previous pursuits would come back. And yesterday morning (waahoo!), I finally felt in control of myself. And I've made progress on many of my projects.

So the moral of the story: keep breathing. And viruses can take out of you more than physical energy. Their effects can linger even after physical energy has returned. Be kind to yourself. Listen to yourself. Apparently I still needed a different sort of rest to recover fully.

Chronic Pain and Illness

Chronic pain and illness can make us feel isolated and helpless. If you have someone to talk to, it can help tremendously. Check the Internet to see if there are support groups for what you are trying to cope with.

Disease is what is happening to the physical body. You can be cured of the symptoms of the disease, but what the illness did to your life may not be healed. Practicing the many tools in this book will help restore balance and resilience in your life. Adopting a holistic wellness paradigm in which we balance, integrate and harmonize the physical, intellectual, emotional and spiritual aspects of the human condition -- that's how healing happens.

Check out the "How To Cope With Pain" website: http://www.howtocopewithpain.org/ for additional help and resources. Keep moving. Tai chi through the Arthritis Foundation and medical yoga are safe, effective ways of staying active and coping with pain.

Also, the National Center for Complementary and Alternative Medicine website is a wonderful resource to help determine what can be helpful in your situation.

A Word About Grief

Grieving is a normal process. It is emotional suffering due to loss. The more significant the loss, the more intense the grieving is likely to be. Any loss however, can cause grief, including:

- Loss of health for self or a loved one
- Losing a job, home, independence
- Death of a pet
- Loss of a dream
- Loss of a friendship or significant relationship
- Loss of safety after a trauma

Everyone grieves differently, and at his own pace. Ignoring the grieving process is a sure recipe for burnout.

The five stages of grief that Elisabeth Kübler-Ross introduced are denial, anger, bargaining, depression and acceptance. They are helpful in understanding our emotional journey when grieving but were never intended to define everyone's grieving process. "Our grieving is as individual as our lives." (Kubler-Ross). Some people may resolve their grieving and go straight to acceptance; others may revisit various stages at times in their journey.

Caring for our Pain

» Embrace your pain with mindfulness. Focus on the area and breathe as if to breathe into it. Visualize cradling, soothing it.
» Each time your pain comes into consciousness, it will be a little weaker from having been embraced by mindfulness.

Practice mindfulness like a mother tenderly embracing your pain. Maintain mindfulness for 5 to10 minutes -- you will experience some relief right away.

Adapted from *True Love*, by Thich Nhat Hanh

Another model of the stages of grieving lists seven stages:
1. Shock and denial.
2. Pain and guilt.
3. Anger and bargaining.
4. Depression, reflection, loneliness.
5. The upward turn.
6. Reconstruction and working through.
7. Acceptance and hope.

Again, these are helpful in gaining insight, but everyone's journey will be different.

Find support: friends, family or a support group can help. Eat healthy, get sleep and exercise. Maintain balance in your life. Know when to seek help. An article on the helpguide.org website says that you should contact a grief counselor or professional therapist if you:
- Feel that life isn't worth living.
- Wish you had died with your loved one.
- Blame yourself for the loss or for failing to prevent it.
- Feel numb and disconnected from others for more than a few weeks.
- Are having difficulty trusting others since your loss.
- \Are unable to perform your normal daily activities.

(Adapted from : Coping with Grief and Loss: Understanding the Grieving Process. Retrieved from http://helpguide.org/mental/grief_loss.htm, 7/15/12.)

Grief: An emotional roller coaster that does not always run in the same direction.

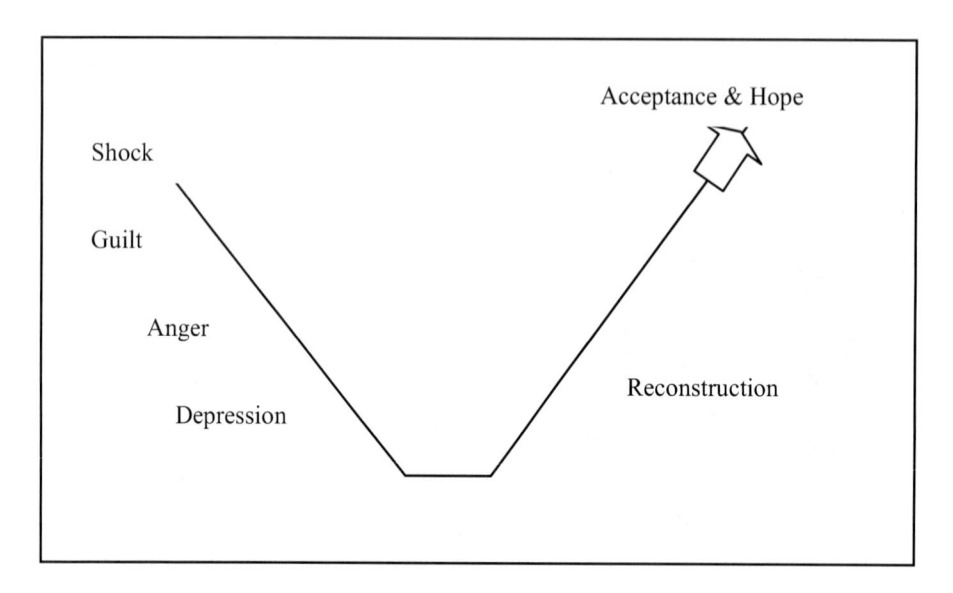

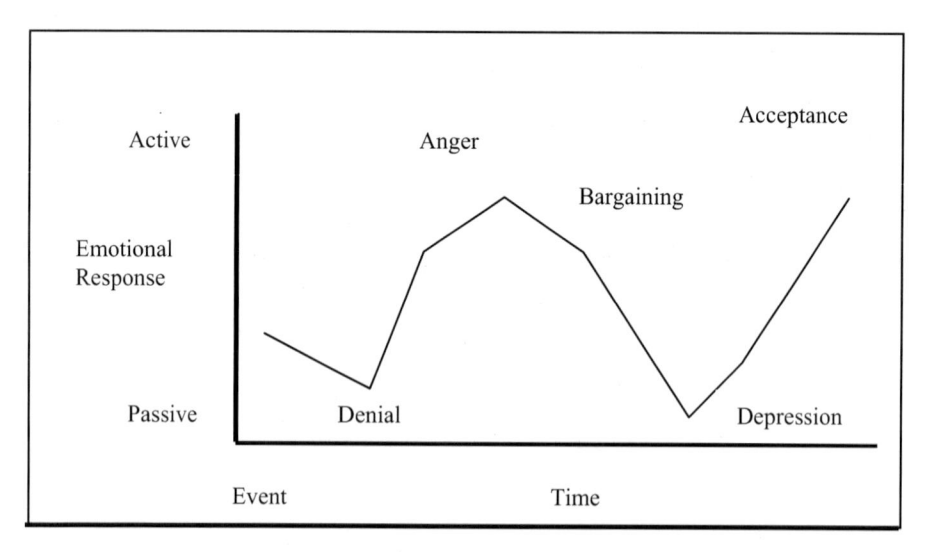

Shock
Guilt
Anger
Depression

Acceptance & Hope
Reconstruction

Active
Emotional Response
Passive

Denial
Anger
Bargaining
Acceptance
Depression

Event   Time

Section V

Are We There Yet?

OF SPECIAL NOTE......

So, what have we learned? To be happy, we need to work all the angles, approach this holistically if we are to have lasting happiness and expel all our boggarts. A healthy diet and appropriate/adequate exercise (self-care) are needed. Eliminate recreational drugs and profoundly limit alcohol. Strive for love and compassion. We've also established that play is important. Play and work are a large part of our life and add considerably to our sense of purpose and fulfillment.

Chapter 15
TAKING ACTION

> "No more would I stay in a safe, predictable routine that made me miserable. Predictability is a trap and safety is an illusion. Love and happiness, on the other hand, are real, but you don't find them without taking chances."
>
> <u>The New Year's Quilt</u>, Jennifer Chiaverini

This chapter is a call to action! Start thinking joy. Don't worry. Be happy. Don't give yourself excuses. You have the tools, you have the resolve and now is the time to JUST DO IT.

The following is an outline of some of the key concepts when you're changing a habit:

1. Motivation
    a. Define a clear purpose
    b. Redefine your purpose to maintain fire and passion
2. Feeling of achievement
    a. Reward yourself...your brain must feel endorphins
    b. Success becomes easier each time
    c. Try and try and try again, changing something each time
    d. Enjoy the challenge
       Ex.: reducing cholesterol -- find a diet and exercise that you enjoy
3. Cues: notecards and reminders
    a. It takes 30 days to make/change a habit
    b. Action plan: keep it simple
    c. Each time we retry, change gets easier. Neuro-pathways are being forged. Each attempt brings rewards and progress

And What Do We Gain?

A clear mind
- » The ability to act instead of react.
- » The ability to make better decisions.

A loving heart
- » This is our true nature/our true identity.
- » Seek first to understand...walk a mile in the other person's shoes. Remember, if whatever is happening does not grow out of love, it is fear-driven.
- » Practice random acts of kindness.
- » Be the first to say, "I'm sorry" and make amends when needed.
- » Every breath is prayer...make every breath count.

Remember
- » Practice holistic stress management techniques: coping and relaxation strategies -- laughter, healthy diet, exercise and, above all, balance.
- » Practice meditation, create a sanctuary for yourself.
- » Harmony of thought and action...do the right thing.
- » Remember: you become that which you think about.

I Have Come Full Circle

My mother's words of wisdom -- maybe they weren't so empty. Grim, yes. Incomplete, yes. But the realization dawns that maybe my mother was smarter than I knew (there's an original thought), however cryptic.

1. Life is tough, then you die.

    Maybe the message was meant to be: Buck up, adapt or change. You have a choice, you can change your attitude and choose happiness. If you choose to internalize this adage, then you're already dead.

2. "Just make sure it's not lust."

    Maybe the message was meant to be: Make it about love.

3.) Ask yourself: "What's the worst that can happen?"

    Maybe the message was meant to be: Be fearless…you can handle that.

> Make it about love, not fear.

In writing this book for my daughter and her husband, as I write these words, I realize that I have found my mother again.

Chapter 16
THE FRUITS OF LIVING WELL
Stories and Words of Wisdom

> JOY IS A SPIRITUAL PRACTICE

You become what you think about…so think joy. Maintain an attitude of gratitude.

PRACTICE CONSCIOUS BEING.
Cultivate that which brings you joy and you will naturally be joyful.

Choose joy daily.

Happiness and Joy

> Happiness is not something that happens to people, but something they make happen.
>
> *Mihaly Csikszentmihalyi*

Joy is a spiritual practice. Here we are again, still taking care of ourselves:
- Practice being happy.
- Our bodies function better when we're happy, and we are more productive/creative when we're happy. We can love others better: "If we are peaceful, if we are happy, we can smile and blossom like a flower, and everyone in our family, our entire society, will benefit from our peace"

Thich Nhat Hanh, Essential Writings..

- The earth is a reflection of heaven.

Tao Te Ching

Therefore, happiness and joy are a spiritual way of life.

It may be as Seligman says: "We're all born with a relatively fixed natural range of well-being imprinted on our genes. Some of us tilt toward the gloomy end of the spectrum, others toward the cheery end. But all of us can learn how to reach the upper portions of our individual range—where happiness can ensue. Among the things that contribute to happiness…are engaging in satisfying work, avoiding negative events and emotions, being married and having a rich social network. Also important are gratitude, forgiveness and optimism. (What doesn't seem to matter much at all, according to the research, are making more money, getting lots of education or living in a pleasant climate.)"

> There is no deep, dark secret to happiness….
> the [only] secret is that it is a choice.
> *"This Emotional Life," program on PBS, 2010*

It is perhaps apropos that I am writing this today. Here as I pick up the threads of the book again (after seven months of working six to seven days per week and preparing for my daughter's wedding), my daughter was married on a Saturday and moved 2,200 miles away the following Monday. I am myself at a crossroads in life, an empty-nester, a mother-in-law, my only child far away (thank heavens for Skype). Happiness is a choice, and though my blood pressure is in the higher range this week and I occasionally tear up at the thought of her being so far from home, I am at peace and know that I am simply out of practice with happiness on my own. But still, what do I do with the rest of my life, what will it look like? For 24 years I have been a mom. What's next?

The best gift I can give them (besides this book, filled with unsolicited advice) is to be happy myself. Balance will reestablish itself, the joy will become a matter of course.

Essential elements of happiness
» Optimism
» Can-do attitude

» Playfulness
» Connectedness

<u>The Childhood Roots of Adult Happiness</u>, Edward M. Hallowell

Love and Connectedness

> Relationships are a place where the greatest emotional and spiritual growth can occur, if we learn to use them for that purpose.
>
> Mindful Loving

> "Anytime we feel a need for love, all we need to do is to extend it and we will experience love—inside of us, not something separate from us....When we are present with whatever is happening, we no longer feel needy."
>
> Mindful Loving

...**WAAHOO!!!!!** This present moment is perfect.
It holds everything I need!

Peace and Calm

Emotional tranquility: positive, peaceful emotions within us and toward those around us.

> [When] we feel mentally resilient and we can cope much better with whatever life offers us, as well as better support others.
>
> (Mental Resilience)

A clear mind gives us the ability to act instead of react -- e.g., to make better decisions. It has been found that when we're stressed, our peripheral vision narrows. Similarly, we problem solve less creatively...we literally see fewer options.

Harmony and Contentment

> "Contentment is not the fulfillment of what you want, but the realization of how much you already have."
>
> *Anonymous*

You are grounded in reality and you have enough. Harmony and joy grow out of the practices of mindfulness...peace, love, kindness. The practices of balance and simplicity lead to empowerment and connectedness.

Enough

Practice enoughness. Why do we need excess if we have enough? This is not just enough to pay the bills but enough to satisfy the frills our hearts desire (in moderation). Besides books, which I can indulge in at the library, my one frill is my wanderlust. I realized a lifelong dream in 2004 and spent a month traveling in Europe with my daughter, and in 2007, I went to England with my Dad and daughter. I hope to do more traveling, but I balance it against my other joys and priorities. If I have the opportunity to do so again, I will be delighted. If not, I will still be delighted with the choices I make in how to spend my time and money. Oh, yes, and then there's yarn....

Confidence and Empowerment

> Courage is resistance to fear, mastery of fear - not absence of fear.
>
> *Mark Twain*

> Courage is not the absence of fear, but rather the judgment that something else is more important than fear.
>
> *Ambrose Redmoon*

> Courage is not the absence of fear, but the conquest of it.
>
> *Author Unknown*

Joel: A Story of Faith * Gratitude * Friendship

Joel Mpabwanimana is from the Democratic Republic of the Congo (DRC). Though his name means "Gift of God," he never felt that the ministry was his calling -- he wanted to be a soldier. At the age of 8 he became very ill from a chemical poison he was accidentally given in a drink. He was ill for two years, missing school until one day he was miraculously healed

"My parents always gave me positive feedback. Because of their wonderful words, I always planned to be somebody and have a big idea, bigger than myself. I always look through my eyes to the future. My wonderful mother always told me good stories about being blessed if I would be obedient. She quoted Deuteronomy 28: 13. "The Lord will make you the head and not the tail if you pay attention to the commands of the Lord your God that I give you this day and carefully follow them. You will always be at the top never at the bottom." These words remain in my mind even today. With the challenges I faced, I could not be who I am today if it were not God's plans. I am who my name means and I thank my parents for naming me such a beautiful and meaningful name.

At 19 he was called to be a teacher and evangelist for the Seventh-day Adventist Church in Rwanda. He left his family and began the ministry. One year later Joel received a call to join the Rwandese army. Excited for the call, Joel prepared himself to go to Belgium where he would receive training for seven years. One night, a month before he was deployed to Belgium for training, a group of gangs attacked him in his house and threatened to cut his head off. Joel states, "A miracle happened that night. God gave me a second chance to live." That night (July 15, 1981, at 2:00 a.m.), Joel made a covenant with his God. He bargained with

God, saying, "If you save me from being killed by these gangs, I would serve you the rest of my life." After Joel's short and silent prayer, he was left for dead. After that, he took to heart the meaning of his name, "Gift of God."

In 1994, Joel and his family were in Nigeria for education. In April, civil war broke out. On April 7th, they were to return to Rwanda by way of the International Airport of Kanombe/Kigali/Rwanda. The airplane that transported the presidents of Rwanda and Burudi was shot down in Kigali/Rwanda that evening. Joel and his family had been unable to leave Nigeria because their passports were missing. Many people died that night at the airport. Again, his life was spared.

When his children were 4 and 8, another civil war began in DRC. Joel was separated from his wife and children. Two years later he was joined by his wife, but both of their children were still missing.

In 1999, Joel and his wife escaped from Kinshasa to the United States. Their escape was another miracle. Many times Joel had been threatened with death by militants and ruling party soldiers. Then a man whom Joel calls an angel rescued him and his wife, sending them to Andrews University in Michigan. They arrived at Andrews University in June of 1999, but they never gave up hope of being reunited with their children.

In 2000, they had news of the children from the American Red Cross. In September Joel returned to Nairobi/Africa where he met his children. At the Nairobi Airport, his son knew him, but his daughter, now 8, was convinced her parents were dead. Over the ensuing months he tried various means, including hours spent talking to his daughter across fencing to trigger her memory. And at the same time he spent much time going back and forth to the U.S. embassy in

Nairobi to get his children released to him (they had no documents). Finally, he convinced his daughter that he really was her biological father.

"Being reunited brought to me a new sense of being really blessed, and that is exactly what my name means. This was another fulfillment of God's promise to me. I will never forsake my children."

The saddest challenges were yet to come. In 2004, after three years of working for an organization, he lost his job because he refused to work on Saturday, his day of worship. At the same time he and his wife were having serious marital problems, which ended up in separation, then a divorce. He lost his job and his wife left him with two small children. This was the saddest moment in his life. However, he always recalled his mother's words of encouragement: "The Lord will make you the head and not the tail... you will always be on top, never on the bottom." These words reassured his future and hopes, and he never gave up.

After he lost his job, his car and home were repossessed. He lost everything. The departure of his wife made everything worse. His family was totally broken, and his ministry totally affected. His children, who were missing for four years, were now going to miss their parenting relationship forever. The joy of being a family was gone. The situation was devastating. He had to deal with the reality and accept it and begin a new life with his children.

"Even though the situation was horrible, I never missed that I am Mpabwanimana, "Gift of God." I believed that even in midst of pain and suffering I should find a room of peace with God. I recalled God's promise in my life. I had my children with me and they gave me hope that everything could be fine. I went on my knees and cried to my father, who promised me a future and hope. During these difficult moments, I kept God's promises and focused on my goals. God was and is still on my side." In September 2005, he moved from Berrien Springs, Mich., to Saginaw, Mich. where he decided to take training classes for chaplaincy. For two years he was a full-time student and full-time parent. "It was by God's grace, my children and I achieved our goals. I believed in God's plans for me."

Now, his son is in college and his daughter is finishing high school. Both are good basketball players and are doing great. In addition to his two Master's degree from Andrews University, he also achieved his chaplaincy education and is a board certified chaplain working full time at St. Joseph's Hospital and Medical Center in Phoenix, Ariz.

Joel's gratitude is unfailing: "I cannot finish before thanking all friends and my church for being close to me and helpful during these hard moments. Your prayers were heard. I am very thankful to my colleagues at Covenant Health Care, and St. Mary's Hospital and Medical Center in Saginaw, Michigan. They mean a lot to me. May God bless you. To both my children, I pray that God will help achieve your future and you will be who God wants you to be. I thank God for giving me good children, they were my best friends. Thanks to my mother, father and siblings, you gave support when needed.

"Above all, to God be the glory. He never failed to fulfill His promises. He blessed me, and I will serve Him until I die."

Bob: A Story of Resilience

One of the most amazing stories I have ever heard was that of Bob Shumaker's experiences as a POW for eight years. He relays the following. "Three of those years were spent in solitary confinement. I am often asked how I and my fellow POWs in Vietnam were able not only to survive the experience but go on to resume normal lives.

"The worst thing I and my fellow POWs could have done under the circumstances would have been to clam up and withdraw. " They developed a tap code, talking about anything from relationships, to elaborate meals, to the house they were going to build when they got home. They focused on supporting each other and dreaming. It was important to them to just know there was a fellow American sharing their experience.

Bob's recommendation to us is, "When things look bleak for you my advice is to *talk* over your problems with your family and friends, *seize control* over as much of your circumstances as possible, and *dream* of a better tomorrow. It worked for me. And if you learn the "tap code" you and I might even support each other no matter how thick the barrier between us."

Alice: A Story of Passion

I'd like you to meet a friend of mine. I met Alice in 1995. Petite, with masses of fluffy white hair, she walked with a slow but firm step. Even then, you saw a woman who had shrunken from her original 5-foot, 6-inch height to a mere 5 feet tall, she was so stooped that it made your back ache just to look at her. Thirteen years later, at the age of 97, she was wrinkled and wizened, her skin paper thin, her hands deeply blue veined, and her clothes hung off her as she pushed her walker along.

At this point, many of us feel pity and even fear. But listen to some things Alice said to me two years before she had gone into rehabilitation after breaking a hip, and when I walked into her room that first afternoon, she half whispered to me, "They say I'll be here for six weeks." Then in a firm voice she said, "I'll be out in four." On another visit, Alice commented to me about her fellow residents by saying, "I thought I'd be the oldest one in here…and I am, except for one." She paused and whispered, "But they're all older than me." Later, when we brought her home, I wanted her to have a bag on her walker to carry things such as a telephone so she wouldn't have to get up every time it rang and *I* wouldn't have to feel guilty for calling her. She was having none of it. She described to me "those old ladies" who lined the hallways in the other part of the nursing home, who walked with their heads down and shuffled their feet. They all had bags on their walkers. She said to me, "I practice walking like this every day," and she pushed her head up and straightened her spine as far as it would go.

When I met Alice, I found that she was a master weaver with over 55 years of unquenchable passion for life and weaving, which for her were synonymous. She had woven more than 300 reproduction Civil War-era blankets for the National Parks Service in five to six styles. She would reproduce the wool yarns from the spin of the thread to the dyes, and when there were mistakes in an original item, she reproduced the mistakes. One of her blankets is used by the Smithsonian Institute for authentication purposes, allowing the originals to stay under glass.

Alice wrote and published her first book at the age of 89. At the age of 91 she invented and marketed a weaving device to fit a variety of looms that provides weavers with a number of time-saving and practical solutions to weaving dilemmas. At the age of 94, she had two more books in the works and was being solicited by companies to analyze fabric swatches that had stumped their experts.

Alice was an amazing woman, and I was privileged to enjoy her wry humor as well. There was one summer afternoon when we took a break from sorting through her fabric and clothing collection. We had piles all around us, and she turned to me with her hands clasped in her lap, and said, "Elaine, when does my next life start?" I was half turned towards her, with my head bent low, nearly touching hers...both of us sat there, just grinning at each other, then Alice answered her own question, chortling as she said, "Well, I guess I'd better get busy."

Passion is the word that comes to my mind when I think of Alice. She had an unquenchable zest for weaving and a deep appreciation for the people in her life. Spending time with her was an opportunity to slow down, to step out of the rat race and to just *be*. One time we joked together that with her as a guide, I had discovered the secret to the fountain of youth...passion and young friends. Both of us had again grinned at the obvious...if you're 95 and don't have young friends, what friends do you have?

Then, at 97 years young, Alice embraced another challenge with grace and dignity. We brought her home from the hospital with the help of Hospice Services, and as we settled her in her bed, she said to me, "You know, Elaine, I could resent this, but with you all here...I know it's going to be wonderful. It's going to be beautiful. I've had a wonderful life and many, *many* unexpected privileges and help. It's just...I can't believe it...I just can't fathom it...all the wonderful, *interesting* people."

John Powell, in his book *Fully Human, Fully Alive*, expresses it well for me: "For such people life has the color of joy and the sound of celebration. Their lives are not a perennial funeral procession. Each tomorrow is a new opportunity which is eagerly anticipated...and when such people come to die their hearts will be filled with gratitude for all that has been...for a beautiful and full experience."

I can hear that smile welling up from her heart when she said to me, "It's going to be beautiful."

I wish you passion. I wish you joy.

I wish you will live to be as young as Alice.

Section VI

Appendices

and

Fun Stuff

APPENDIX 1   CHOOSING A THERAPIST

Sometimes we need another set of objective ears to help us sort out our issues and offer guidance as we strive to make changes in our lives. Below are some things to consider when choosing a therapist:

- **Education.** Is she licensed by the state? Credentialed by the American Association for Marriage and Family Therapy (AAMFT)?
- **Experience.** What is his experience with your type of issue -- marriage/couples counseling, anger management, eating disorders, sexual dysfunction, mood disorders, addictions, etc.?
- **Philosophy/approach to treatment. The website for Good Therapy.org** (http://www.goodtherapy.org/types-of-therapy.html) **has an exhaustive list and descriptions of the various types of therapy that are available. Positive therapy is a newer style that focuses on your strengths rather than an exhaustive rehashing of the past.**
- **Logistics.** Location, office hours, availability in case of emergency.
- **Sessions.** Length, how often, how many can you expect, cancellation policy, etc.
- **Fees and insurance.** Charges for each session. Are they covered by health insurance? Are fees paid upfront?
- **What to expect during sessions.** How the counselor interacts with you
- **Diane Browning's article has a list of possible questions.** Prepare your questions ahead of time, see if you can talk briefly with the counselor on the telephone.

The Initial Visit

Your comfort with the counselor/therapist is of first importance. Follow your instincts regarding your comfort level and trust. Is she a good fit? Are you nervous, anxious, do you have any misgivings about her, did you feel listened to? Be sure to separate your feelings about the counselor from your feelings about counseling. Discuss any reservations with the counselor. If after the first visit you determine it is not a good fit, keep looking.

NOTE: Marriage counseling may be helpful in some cases of domestic abuse. However, if you are afraid or have been hurt, counseling isn't adequate. See Appendix 3, make a plan and seek emergency help.

Adapted from:

Browning, Diane, Guidelines for Choosing a Psychotherapist or Counselor, available at http://www.findacounselor.net/therapist-articles.html

Good Therapy.org, available at http://www.goodtherapy.org/types-of-therapy.html

Marriage counseling, available at Mayoclinic.com

Singer, Jack N., Helpful Guidelines for Choosing the Right Therapist, available at http://www.4therapy.com/life-topics/therapists-perspectives/helpful-guidelines-choosing-right-therapist-2782.

Stride Like a Lion, Soar Like an Eagle   221

APPENDIX 2   MASLOW'S HIERARCHY OF HUMAN NEEDS*

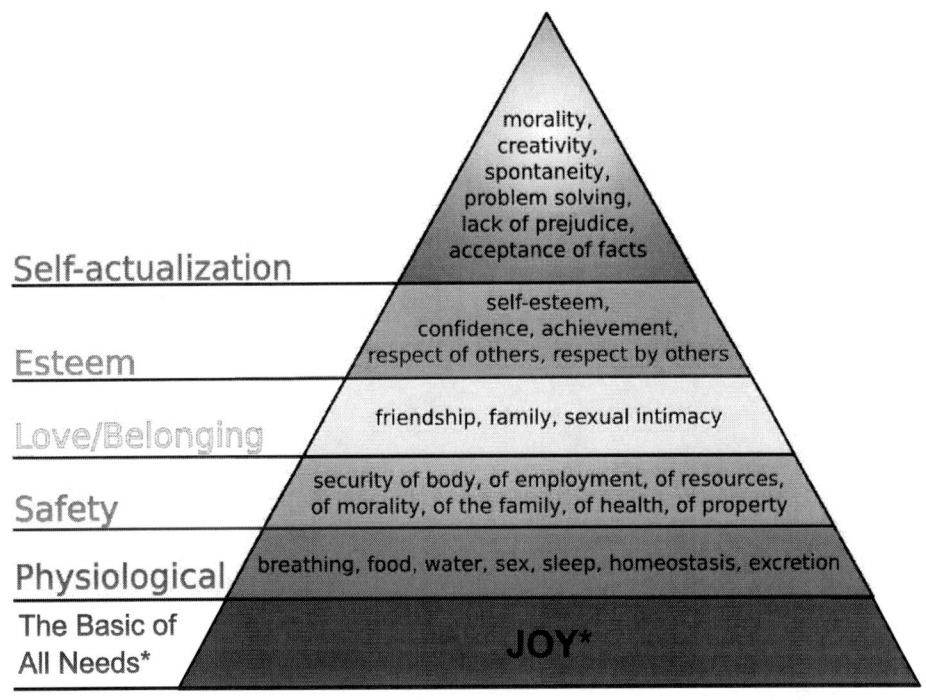

Self-actualization — morality, creativity, spontaneity, problem solving, lack of prejudice, acceptance of facts

Esteem — self-esteem, confidence, achievement, respect of others, respect by others

Love/Belonging — friendship, family, sexual intimacy

Safety — security of body, of employment, of resources, of morality, of the family, of health, of property

Physiological — breathing, food, water, sex, sleep, homeostasis, excretion

The Basic of All Needs* — JOY*

*Adapted by Elaine Scribner, 2009

APPENDIX 3   ABUSIVE RELATIONSHIPS

Salvaging a relationship

» **If it's safe**…be sure to get things right with yourself first. Grayson in *Mindful Loving* has some powerful suggestions that may save your relationship.
» Therapy is a necessary component for lasting change.
» If you do leave this relationship, be sure to get things right with yourself before leaping into another relationship. Otherwise, history tends to repeat itself.

If your situation is not safe, if it is abusive or even dangerous, you need to take action.

The following was adapted from: Recovering Info, Available at http://www.recovery-man.com/abusive/abusive.html

HelpGuide.org, available at http://helpguide.org/mental/domestic_violence_abuse_help_treatment_prevention.htm

U.S. Department of Agriculture, Domestic Violence Awareness Handbook, Available at http://www.dm.usda.gov/shmd/aware.htm

Identifying the abusive relationship: Does the person you love...

- Constantly keep track of your time?
- Act jealous and possessive?
- Accuse you of being unfaithful or flirting?
- Discourage your relationships with friends and family?
- Prevent or discourage you from working, interacting with friends or attending school?
- Constantly criticize or belittle you?
- Control all finances and force you to account for what you spend? (reasonable cooperative budgeting excepted.)
- Humiliate you in front of others? (includes "jokes" at your expense.)

- Destroy or take your personal property or sentimental items?
- Have affairs?
- Threaten to hurt you, your children or pets? Threaten to use a weapon?
- Push, hit, slap, punch, kick or bite you or your children?
- Force you to have sex against your will, or demand sexual acts you are uncomfortable with?

Domestic Violence: Where to Turn for Help

For emergency help: Call 911 if you are in immediate danger of domestic violence or have already been hurt.

For advice and support: Call the National Domestic Violence Hotline at 1-800-799-7233 (SAFE).

Help through email: ndvh@ndvh.org

Help for the hearing-impaired: 1-800-787-3224 (TTY) or deafhelp@ndvh.org

SAFETY ALERT!

Computer use can be monitored, and the use history is impossible to clear completely. If you are afraid your Internet and/or computer usage might be monitored, please use a safer computer and/or call the National Domestic Violence Hotline at **1-800-799-SAFE(7233)** or **TTY 1-800-787-3224.**

For a safe place to stay: Call your state's branch of the National Coalition Against Domestic Violence if you need a shelter from domestic violence.

Domestic Violence and Abuse

If you're a victim of domestic violence or abuse, you may be afraid to seek help because you are afraid of what your partner would do if he found out. However, there are many things you can do to protect yourself when leaving. Start by creating a safety plan ahead of time, so you know exactly where to go and how to get away fast when your abuser attacks. Call the National Domestic Violence Hotline at 1-800-799-7233 (SAFE) for advice and help with your escape.

Getting help for domestic abuse or violence

How can a woman safely leave an abusive relationship and protect herself from further abuse? Most women cannot simply leave their homes, their jobs, their children's schools, their friends and their relatives to escape their abuser. They depend upon police to enforce the law against physical abuse. But police cannot act until a restraining order is violated or until some physical harm is done.

Many victims of domestic violence believe that it's easier to stay with the abuser than to try to leave and risk retaliation. However, there are many things that you can do to protect yourself while getting out of an abusive situation, and there are people waiting to help.

Pack a survival kit:

- Money for cab fare.
- A change of clothes.
- Extra house and car keys.
- Birth certificates.
- Driver's license or passport.
- Medications and copies of prescriptions.
- Insurance information.
- Checkbook.
- Credit cards.
- Legal documents such as separation agreements and protection orders.
- Address book.
- Valuable jewelry.
- Papers that show jointly owned assets.

Conceal it in the home or leave it with a trusted neighbor, friend or relative. Important papers can also be left in a bank deposit box.

Telephone Safety Tips

When seeking help for domestic violence, call from a public pay phone or another phone outside the house, using one of the following payment methods:

- A prepaid phone card.
- A friend's telephone charge card.
- Coins.
- A collect call.

When you seek help by phone, use a corded phone if possible, rather than a cordless phone or cell phone. A corded phone is more private, and harder to tap.

Remember that if you use your own home phone or telephone charge card, the phone numbers that you call may be listed on the monthly bill that is sent to your home.

Even if you've already left by the time the bill arrives, your abuser may be able to track you down by the phone numbers you've called for help.

You can call 911 for free on most public phones, so know where the closest one is in case of emergency. Some domestic violence shelters offer free cell phones to battered women. Call your local hotline to find out more.

Seeking help online safely

If you seek help online, you are safest if you use a computer outside of your home. You can use a computer at a domestic violence shelter or agency, at work, at a friend's house, at a library or at a community center.

It is almost impossible to clear a computer of all evidence of the websites that you have visited unless you know a lot about Internet browsers and about your own computer. Also be careful when sending email -- your abuser may know how to access your account. See the Women's law.org article on Internet security for instructions for covering your online tracks and email history, but be wary of leaving traces that your abuser might find.

Locate a women's shelter:

A domestic violence shelter or *women's shelter* is a building or set of apartments where victims of domestic violence can go to seek refuge from their abusers. The location of the shelter is kept confidential to keep your abuser from finding you.

The domestic violence shelter will provide for all your basic living needs, including food and child care. Shelters generally have room for both mothers and their children. The length of time you can stay at the shelter is limited, but most shelters also help victims find permanent homes, jobs and other things they need to start a new life.

If you go to a domestic violence shelter or women's refuge, you do not have to give identifying information about yourself, even if asked. Shelters take many measures to protect the women they house, but giving a false name may help keep your abuser from finding you (particularly if you live in a small town).

After you leave

Once you have left, safety is just starting. You may need to relocate, change schools, change your routine. Seek help from one of the organizations above.

AFTERWORD AND MOMISMS
Those gems your mom (or dad) said that made you smile, made you think, or simply made you laugh

For beauty I am not a star, there are others more lovely by far, my face I don't mind it, because I'm behind it, it's the people in front that I jar.

Don't cut off your nose to spite your face.

The yellow stream by I. P. Freely.

The spot on the wall by Hu Flung Dung.

Hee, Hee, Hee, Hee......

Yorkshire English (phonetic):
Open ze gob and stick out ze lollicka
(p.s. gob is Gaelic for mouth, lollicka is tounge).

When God gave out noses, I thought He said "roses" and said, "I want a big red one."

Eat your green beans, they make your hair curl.

Mom used to say "just put one foot in front of the other" when things got tough.

Gramma Stanley and mom used to tell us to be careful or we would break our knenobewaddle. I don't know exactly how this old Gaelic word is spelled, but it meant we would break something that should not be broken.

When God gave out brains, I thought He said "trains,"
So I said I would take a short one, please.

To change the subject when the going got tough, or when someone said something off the wall, we would respond: "Aren't the trees beautiful?"

Anne submitted by: Kate, Judy, Liz and Elaine

Don't go out with a wet head, you will catch cold.

It is not that I don't trust you, it is that I don't trust everyone else.

Jayne

Dr. N, Dentist: Patient had a chocolate bar hanging out of her purse…"for stress," she said.

Rosalyn, the Hygienist told her:
"And if that doesn't work have a second one."

Careful or your face will freeze like that.

Linda

A watched pot never boils.

You make a better door than a window.

If you are going to throw snowballs don't get caught!

What comes around goes around.

Beauty is only skin deep.

Put your scarf and mittens on or you'll catch pneumonia.

Sleep tight, don't let the bed bugs bite.

Sticks and stones may break your bones but names will never hurt you.

Always wear clean underwear you never know when you could be in an accident.

Practice makes perfect.

If you don't have anything nice to say, don't say anything at all.

Money doesn't grow trees.

The world does not revolve around you.

Finish your dinner, there are children starving in Africa.

When you're older you'll understand.

Because I said so...

Stand up straight - don't slouch.

Do onto others as you wish to be done to you.

Eat your onions it will make your hair curly.

Just three bites that's all I ask
(this made us learn to eat different foods).

Barb

Don't look at me with that tone of voice.

Sit up straight.

Pour yourself a drink, put some lipstick on and pull yourself together.

Who do you think you are?

You think we're made of money?

Mrs. L

My Mom sang "take good care of yourself you belong to me" every time we left the house. She also said "love one another" when we fought. When things were horrible she would say "life isn't fair".

Beatrice

"Why walk when you can fly"
....title of song by Mary Chapin Carpenter.

Bea

As for any of my mother's sayings, the only one that I can remember that got me to laughing was when I was little and was bathing. My mom wanted to be sure I bathed my whole body, so she said: "Sometimes I wash up as far as possible, and sometimes I wash down as far as possible, and sometimes I even wash possible."

"Would you jump off a bridge just because everyone else did?"

"Close the door -- were you born in a barn?"

"I don't care what everybody else is doing, you're not going to do it."

Bernice

If my mother could see me now, she would stand on her head stacking greased bee-bees.

Coworker in East Texas

Careful, or your face will freeze like that.

Linda

"Voh-che strujx, a ryk: zrobyoum" (phonetic Ukrainian)
Translated: The eyes are scared, but the hands can do it

Mary

From the day you are born
Till the day you ride in the hearse
There's nothing so bad,
But might have been worse.

It's not the fall that hurts you, it's the sudden stop.

First your money,
and then your clothes.
That's the way it goes.

As a rule, a man's a fool
When it's hot he wants it cool
When it's cool, he wants it hot
He's always wanting what it's not.

That's the way the mop flops

When anyone talks about food, I listen.

Bruce

Don't get old unless it's absolutely necessary

Bill

References & Resources

Introduction

His Holiness the Dalai Lama, *How to See Yourself as You Really Are*, Atria, New York, 2006.

Gilman, Dorothy, *Mrs. Pollifax on the China Station*, Fawcett Crest, New York, 1984.

Fries, James F. and Vickery, Donald M., Take Care of Yourself (Sixth Edition), Addison-Wesley Publishing Company, Boston, 1996.

SECTION I.
THE ART OF LIVING WELL

Chapter 1 LIVING WELL

Coyhis, Don, *Medicine Wheel Teachings for Healthy Organizations, Servant Leadership*, Audiotapes, Moh-he-con-nuck, Inc., 1993.

Dyer, Wayne W., *Change Your Thoughts – Change Your Life*, Hay House, Inc., Carlsbad, Calif., 2007 (Tao Te Ching Translation).

Frankl, Viktor E., *Man's Search for Meaning -- An Introduction to Logotherapy*, Pocket Books, New York, 1975.

Maslow. Abraham, A Theory of Human Motivation, Psychological Review 1943, 50(4): 370-96.

Pink, Daniel H., *A Whole New Mind – Why Right-Brainers Will Rule The World*, Riverhead Books, New York, 2005.

Rowling, J.K., *Harry Potter and the Prisoner of Azkaban*, Scholastic Press, 1999.

Seaward, Brian Luke, *Quiet Mind, Fearless Heart, The Taoist Path through Stress and Spirituality*, John Wiley & Sons, Inc., Hoboken, N.J., 2004.

Chapter 2 SPIRITUALITY AND LOVE

Chiaverini, Jennifer, *The New Year's Quilt*, Simon & Schuster, New York, 2007.

Frankl, Viktor E., *Man's Search for Meaning -- An Introduction to Logotherapy*, Pocket Books, New York, 1975.

Grayson, Henry, *Mindful Loving -- 10 Practices for Creating Deeper Connections*, Penguin Group, New York, 2003.

Harder, Arlene F., http://www.learningplaceonline.com/stages/organize/Erikson.htm, Retrieved March 26, 2009.

Kingsolver, Barbara, "The Color Red", the magazine AARP, May & June 2009.

Lander, Eric, cited in Pink, Daniel H., *A Whole New Mind – Why Right-Brainers Will Rule The World*, Riverhead Books, New York, 2005.

Merriam-Webster Online Dictionary, http://www.merriam-webster.com/dictionary/spirit. Retrieved March 14, 2009.

Murray, E., "Coping and Anger", *In Stress and Coping*, T. Field, P. McCabe and N. Schneiderman (editors), Erlbaum, Hillsdale, N.J., 1985.

Pope John Paul II, cited in Pink, Daniel H., *A Whole New Mind – Why Right-Brainers Will Rule The World*, Riverhead Books, New York, 2005.

Pink, Daniel H., *A Whole New Mind – Why Right-Brainers Will Rule The World*, Riverhead Books, New York, 2005.

Reson, James Galieo, "Pope Joan Paul II (Karol Wojtyla), A Life", HarperCollins, New York, 1994, p. 461.

Tavris, C., Anger—*The Misunderstood Emotion*, Simon & Schuster, New York, 1982.

The Holy Bible, King James Version.

SECTION II.
21ST CENTURY TOOLS

A Course In Miracles, (2nd Edition), Foundation for Inner Peace, Mill Valley, Calif., 1992.

"Centered Silliness: Laughing Meditation/Mindful Laughing", Adapted from: Dailyom.com, September 16, 2005.

Seaward, Brian Luke, *Stressed is Desserts Spelled Backward -- Rising Above Life's Challenges with Humor, Hope, and Courage*, Conari Press, Berkeley, Calif., 1999.

Chapter 3 THE POWER OF WORDS

Coyhis, Don, "Medicine Wheel Teachings for Healthy Organizations, Servant Leadership", Audiotapes, Moh-he-con-nuck, Inc., 1993.

Ebbesen, E., Duncan, B., and Konecni V., "Effects of Content of Verbal Agression on Future Verbal Aggression: A Field Experiment", Journal of Experimental Social Psychology 11:192-204, 1975.

Hebert, Dean, "Do You Rebound Or Awfulize?" July 28, 2007 available at http://coachdeanhebert.wordpress.com/2007/07/28/do-you-rebound-or-awfulize/

Gilman, Dorothy, *Incident at Badayma*, Fawcett, New York, 1990.

Grayson, Henry, *Mindful Loving -- 10 Practices for Creating Deeper Connections*, Penguin Group, New York, 2003.

Jampolski, Gerald G. and Cirincione, Diane V., *Change Your Mind, Change your Life*, Bantam Books, New York, 1993.

LaRoche, Loretta, *Relax – You May Only Have a Few Minutes Left*, Villard, New York, 1998.

"Positive Affirmations: The Positive Mindset", website, http://www.vitalaffirmations.com.

Powell, John, *The Secret of Staying in Love -- Loving Relationships through Communication*, Thomas More, Allen, Texas, 1974.

Rowling, J.K., *Harry Potter and the Goblet of Fire*, Scholastic Press, 2000.

Simon, Sidney B. and Simon, Suzanne, *Forgiveness, How to Make Peace With Your Past and Get on With Your Life*, Rational Island Publishers, Seattle, Washington, 1990.

Steiner, Claude M., *Scripts People Live -- Transactional Analysis of Life Scripts*, Bantam, New York, 1974.

Thich Nhat Hanh, (translated by Sherab Chodzin Kohn), *True Love*, Shambhala, Boston, 2004.

Chapter 4 THE POWER OF SPIRITUALITY

Artress, Lauren, *Walking a Sacred Path -- Rediscovering the Labyrinth as a Spiritual Tool*, Riverhead Books, New York, 1995.
Anand, Margot, *The Art of Everyday Ecstasy*, Broadway Books, New York, 1998.
Bhagavad-Gita Trust 1998 - 2009 U.S.A., available at http://www.bhagavad-gita.org/Gita/verse-04-18.html, Retrieved August 12, 2012.
Dyer, Wayne W., *Change Your Thoughts – Change Your Life*, Hay House, Inc., Carlsbad, Calif., 2007 (Tao Te Ching Translation).
Gilbert, Elizabeth, *Eat, Pray, Love: One Woman's Search for Everything Across Italy, India and Indonesia*, The Penguin Group, New York, NY, 2006.
Pink, Daniel H., *A Whole New Mind – Why Right-Brainers Will Rule The World*, Riverhead Books, New York, 2005.
Sarma, Kamal, *Mental Resilience, The Power of Clarity, How to Develop the Focus of a Warrior and the Peace of a Monk*, New World Library, Novato, Calif., 2008.
Thich Nhat Hanh, (translated by Sherab Chodzin Kohn), *True Love*, Shambhala, Boston, 2004.
Thich Nhat Hanh, *Essential Writings*, edited by Robert Ellsberg, Orbis Books, Maryknoll, New York, 2001.

Chapter 5 THE POWER OF LOVE

Bhagavad-Gita Trust 1998 - 2009 U.S.A., available at http://www.bhagavad-gita.org/Gita/verse-04-18.html, Retrieved August 12, 2012.

COMPASSION

Bramson, Robert M., *Coping with Difficult People*, Ballantine, New York, 1981.
Buss, D.M., *The Evolution of Desire: Strategies of Human Mating*, Basic Books, New York, 2003.
Christakis, Nicholas A. and Fowler, James H., *Connected: The Surprising Power of Our Social Networks and How They Shape Our Lives -- How Your Friends' Friends' Friends Affect Everything You Feel, Think, and Do*, Little, Brown and Company, New York, NY, 2009.

Cohen, Stephen, *When the Going Gets Rough: Best Strategies for a Job Going Sour*, Bantam Books, 1987.
Grayson, Henry, *Mindful Loving -- 10 Practices for Creating Deeper Connections*, Penguin Group, New York, 2003.
Kennedy, Marilyn Moats, *Office Warfare: Strategies for Getting Ahead in the Aggressive 80's*, Mass Market Paperbacks, 1986.
Roberts, Wess, *Leadership Secrets of Attila the Hun*, Warner Books, New York, 1985.
Worthington, Everett L., *The Power of Forgiving*, Templeton Foundation Press, Penn., 2005.

KINDNESS

Buss, D.M., *The Evolution of Desire: Strategies of Human Mating*, Basic Books, New York, 2003.
Heller, Scott, "Emerging Field Of Forgiveness Studies Explores How We Let Go Of Grudges." The Chronicle of Higher Education Archives, article dated July 17, 1998.
Ferrucci, Piero, (translated by Vivien Reid Ferrucci), *The Power of Kindness -- The Unexpected Benefits of Leading a Compassionate Life*, Penguin Group, New York, 2006.
Herman, M.A. and McHale, S.M., "Coping with Parental Negativity: Links with Parental Warmth and Child Adjustment." Journal of Applied Developmental Psychology 14 (1993):121-36.
Russek, Linda G. and Schwartz, Gary E., "Feelings of Parental Caring Predict Health Status in Midlife: A 35-Year Follow-up of the Harvard Mastery of Stress Study", Journal of Behavioral Medicine, Vol. 20, No. 1, 1997.
Sarma, Kamal, *Mental Resilience, The Power of Clarity -- How to Develop the Focus of a Warrior and the Peace of a Monk*, New World Library, Novato, Calif., 2008.
Simon, Sidney B. and Simon, Suzanne, *Forgiveness -- How to Make Peace With Your Past and Get on With Your Life*, Rational Island Publishers, Seattle, Washington, 1990.

FORGIVENESS

Berry, Jack W. and Worthington Jr., Everett L., "Forgivingness, relationship quality, stress while imagining relationship events, and physical and mental health", Journal of Counseling Psychology Vol 48(4) (Oct 2001), 447-455.

Enright, Robert, (Heller, Scott, Chronicle of Higher Education, July 17,1998), available at http://troy.troy.edu/organizations/leadership_tips/tips/howtoforgive.htm.

Kraybill, Donald B., Nolt, Steven M., and Weaver-Zercher, David L., "Amish Grace: How Forgiveness Transcended Tragedy", Jossey-Bass, 2007.

Kraybill, Donald B., Nolt, Steven M., and Weaver-Zercher, David L., "Amish Grace and the Rest of Us". Christianity Today, September 17, 2007, available at http://www.christianitytoday.com/ct/2007/septemberweb-only/138-13.0.html. Retrieved 2008-01-17.

Lawler, K.A., Younger, J.W., Piferi, R.L., Jobe, R.L., Edmondson, K.A., and Jones, W.H., "The Unique Effects Of Forgiveness On Health: An Exploration Of Pathways", Journal of Behavioral Medicine, 28(2)(April 2005): 157-67.

Lawler, K.A., Younger, J.W., Piferi, R.L., Billington, E., Jobe, R., Edmondson, K., and Jones, W.H., "A Change Of Heart: Cardiovascular Correlates Of Forgiveness In Response To Interpersonal Conflict", Journal Behavioral Medicine, 26(5) (October 2003): 373-93.

Piderman, Katherine M., "Forgiveness: How to let go of grudges and bitterness", Retrieved from www.mayoclinic.com May 16, 2009.

Sarma, Kamal, *Mental Resilience, The Power of Clarity -- How to Develop the Focus of a Warrior and the Peace of a Monk*, New World Library, Novato, Calif., 2008.

Seaward, Brian Luke, *Quiet Mind, Fearless Heart, The Taoist Path through Stress and Spirituality*, John Wiley & Sons, Inc., Hoboken, N.J., 2004.

Tutu, Desmond, *No Future Without Forgiveness*, Doubleday, New York, NY, 1999.

Chapter 6 BALANCE

SIMPLICITY

Dyer, Wayne W., *Change Your Thoughts – Change Your Life*, Hay House, Inc., Carlsbad, Calif., 2007 (Tao Te Ching Translation).

St. James, Elaine, *Inner Simplicity: 100 ways to regain peace and nourish your soul*, Hyperion Publishing, New York, 1995.

SLEEP

"Can't Sleep? What To Know About Insomnia", National Sleep Foundation, available at: http://www.sleepfoundation.org/article/sleep-related-problems/insomnia-and-sleep.

Maas, James B., *Power Sleep -- The Revolutionary Program That Prepares Your Mind for Peak Performance*, Quill, Minneapolis, 2001.

MacFarlane, Muriel, *Getting a Good Night's Sleep, Natural Solutions for Sleep Disorders*, United Research Publishers, Encinitas, Calif., 2005., available at www.sleepfoundation.org.

WORK

Blanchard, Ken, Carlos, John P., and Randolph, Alan, *Empowerment Takes More Than a Minute*, Berrett-Koehler Publishers, San Francisco, Calif., 1996.

Blanchard, Kenneth and Johnson, Spencer, *The One Minute Manager*, Berkley Books, New York, 1981.

Blanchard, Kenneth and Peale, Norman Vincent, *The Power of Ethical Management*, Fawcett Crest, New York, 1988.

Blanchard, Kenneth, Oncken Jr., William, and Burrows, Hal, *The One Minute Manager Meets the Monkey*, Quill William Morrow, New York, 1989.

Covey, Stephen R., *The 7 Habits of Highly Effective People -- Powerful Lessons in Personal Change*, Simon & Schuster, New York, 1989.

Covey, Stephen R., *Principle-Centered Leadership*, Simon & Schuster, New York, 1990.

Feigelson, Sheila, *Energize Your Meetings with Laughter*, Association for Supervision and Curriculum Development, Alexandria, Virginia, 1998.

Leigh, Edward. "Making Work Fun", available at http://www.edwardleigh.com/articles/features/humor.html.

Pine, J. and Gilmore, J., *The Experience Economy*, Harvard Business School Press, Boston, Mass.,1999.

Wilson, Steve, *PWLOARYK: The Art of Mixing Work and Play*, Applied Humor Systems, 1992.

MONEY MATTERS

Orman, Suze, website available at suzeorman.com.

EXERCISE

Mayo Clinic, available at www.mayoclinic.com, (search for Target Heart Rate Calculator).

American College of Sports Medicine, ACSM Guidelines – FITT principle (frequency, intensity, time and type) of exercise, available at www.acsm.org.

Tai Chi classes: The Arthritis Foundation.

The health benefits of Tai Chi, retrieved April 5, 2011. http://www.health.harvard.edu/newsletters/Harvard_Womens_Health_Watch/2009/May/The-health-benefits-of-tai-chi?utm_source=womens&utm_medium=pressrelease&utm_campaign=womens0509.

NUTRITION . . . CHANGING HABITS

Foco, Zonya, "Diet Free", available at http://www.zonya.com/ and http://www.dietfree.com/

My Pyramid, available at www.mypyramid.gov

LAUGHTER AND PLAY

"Centered Silliness: Laughing Meditation/Mindful Laughing", Sept. 16, 2005, available at www.Dailyom.com.

Berk, Lee, et al., "Neuroendocrine and Stress Hormone Changes During Mirthful Laughter" American Journal of the Medical Sciences, vol.298, no.6, 1989.

Boyadjian, Berge, *Create Fun At Work: Improve Your Productivity, Quality of Life, and the Morale of Those Around You*, Knowledge Capture and Transfer, Long Beach, Calif., 1999.

Brooks, Joan, "To Know How to Play is Vital to the New Economy", The Algoma News, March 14, 2012., available at http://www.thealgomanews.ca.

"Laughing – How serious is that?" Retrieved Dec. 15, 2011, available at http://rmcpl.wordpress.com/2011/08/22/cl-laughing-how-serious-is-that/.

Collinson, David L., "Managing Humour," Journal of Management Studies, Vol 39, Issue 3, pgs. 269-288 (May 2002).

Feigelson, Sheila, *Energize Your Meetings with Laughter*, Association for Supervision and Curriculum Development, Alexandria, Virginia, 1998.

Fry, William, "Mirth and the Human Cardiovascular System." *The Study of Humor*. Antioch University Press, Los Angeles, Calif., 1979.

Goodheart, Annette, *Laughter Therapy -- How to Laugh About Everything in Your Life That Isn't Really Funny*, Less Stress Press, Santa Barbara, Calif., 1994.

Isen, A.M.. "Missing in Action in the AIM: Positive Affect's Facilitation of Cognitive Flexibility, Innovation, and Problem Solving." Psychological Inquiry 13(1): 57-65 (2002).

Laughter yoga classes – find a class by visiting laughteryoga.org.

Pink, Daniel H., *A Whole New Mind – Why Right-Brainers Will Rule The World*, Riverhead Books, New York, 2005.

Sala, Fabio, "Laughing All the Way to the Bank," Harvard Business Review, Sept 2003.

"Serious Play", available at http://www.seriousplay.com/.

Sittenfeld, Curtis, "He's No Fool (But He Plays One Inside Companies)", available at http://www.fastcompany.com/35777/hes-no-fool-he-plays-one-inside-companies, published Oct 31, 1998., retrieved Aug 12, 2012.

Wilson, Steve, *The Art of Mixing Work and Play*, Applied Humor Systems, Steve Wilson Publishing Company, Columbus, Ohio, 1992.

Wooten, Patty, *Compassionate Laughter, Jest for Your Life*, Jest Press, Santa Cruz, Calif., 2002.

STRONG EMOTIONAL REACTIONS

Frey, William, *Crying: The Mystery of Tears*, Winston Press, Texas, 1977.

Pink, Daniel H., *A Whole New Mind – Why Right-Brainers Will Rule The World*, Riverhead Books, New York, 2005.

Seaward, Brian Luke, *Managing Stress, Principles and Strategies for Health and Well-Being*, (Sixth Edition), Jones and Bartlett Publishers, Boston, 2009.

Skorucak A., "The Science of Tears", available at www.ScienceIQ.com. Accessed Sept 29, 2006.

Section III.
RELATIONSHIPS

Chapter 7 RELATIONSHIP WITH SELF: BEING . . . HAPPY AND WHOLE

Arenson, Gloria, *Five Simple Steps to Emotional Healing: The Last Self-Help Book You Will Ever Need*, Simon & Schuster, New York, 2001.

Cloud, Henry and Townsend, John, *Boundaries: When to Say YES, When to Say NO, To Take Control of Your Life*, Zondervan, Grand Rapids, MI, 1992.

Fowler, James H. and Christakis, Nicholas A., "Dynamic spread of happiness in a large social network: longitudinal analysis over 20 years in the Framingham Heart Study", Retrieved from: BMJ 2008; 337 doi: 10.1136/bmj.a2338 (Published 4 December 2008).

Grayson, Henry, *Mindful Loving -- 10 Practices for Creating Deeper Connections*, Penguin Group, New York, 2003.

Lerner, Harriet Goldhor, *The Dance of Anger -- A Woman's Guide to Changing the Patterns of Intimate Relationships*, Harper Row Publishers, New York, 1985.

Lerner, Harriet Goldhor, *The Dance of Intimacy -- A Woman's Guide to Courageous Act of Change in Key Relationships*, Harper & Row Publishers, New York, 1989.

Radcliffe, Ann, quoting from *The Mysteries of Udolpho*, 1764.

Thich Nhat Hanh, (translated by Sherab Chodzin Kohn), *True Love*, Shambhala, Boston, 2004.

Thich Nhat Hanh, *Essential Writings*, Orbis Books, Maryknoll, New York, 2001.

Tillich, Paul, *The Courage to Be*, The Colonial Press Inc., Clinton, Mass., 1972.

Tolle, Eckhart, *A New Earth, Awakening to Your Life's Purpose*, Penguin Group, New York, 2005.
Vanzant, Iyanla, *Living Through the Meantime, Learning to Break the Patterns of the Past and Begin the Healing Process*, Simon and Schuster, New York, 2001.

Chapter 8 RELATIONSHIP WITH THE DIVINE

Covey, Stephen R., *The 7 Habits of Highly Effective People -- Powerful Lessons in Personal Change*, Simon & Schuster, New York, 1989.
Covey, Stephen R., *Principle-Centered Leadership*, Simon & Schuster, New York, 1990.
Peck, M. Scott, *Further Along the Road Less Traveled: The Unending Journey Toward Spiritual Growth*, Simon and Schuster, New York, 1993.
Peck, M. Scott, *The Road Less Traveled, A New Psychology of Love,Traditional Values and Spiritual Growth*, Simon and Schuster, New York, 1978.

Chapter 9 FAMILY RELATIONSHIPS

Bradshaw, John, *The Family, A Revolutionary Way of Self-Discovery*, Health Communications, Inc., Deerfield Beach, Florida, 1988.
Butler, Susan, *Non-Competitive Games for People of All Ages*, Bethany House, Minneapolis, 1986.
Dyer, Wayne W., *Change Your Thoughts – Change Your Life*, Hay House, Inc., Carlsbad, Calif., 2007 (Tao Te Ching Translation).
Dobson, James, *Dare to Discipline*, Tyndale House Publishers, Wheaton, Ill, 1970.
Family Education Center, available at http://www.familyeducationcenter.com/Fmeetings.htm.
Hallowell, Edward M., *The Childhood Roots of Adult Happiness*, Random House, New York, 2002.
Lansky, Vicki, *101 Ways to Make Your Child Feel Special*, Contemporary Books, Inc., Chicago, Ill, 1991.
Mendler, Allen N., *Smiling At Yourself: Educating Young Children About Stress And Self-Esteem*, ETR Associates, Calif., 1990.
Nelson, Ed and Jane, D., *Positive Discipline*, Ballatine Books, New York, 1991.

Pantell, Robert H., Fries, James F., and Vickery, Donald. M., *Take Care of Yourself*, (Revised Edition), Addison-Wesley Publishing Company, Boston, 1984.

Parenting classes are great resources.

Powell, John, *The Secret of Staying in Love -- Loving Relationships through Communication*, Thomas More, Allen, Texas, 1974.

Schaef, Anne Wilson, *Native Wisdom for White Minds, Daily Reflections Inspired by the Native Peoples of the World*, Ballantine Books, New York, 1995.

Zen Habits, available at http://zenhabits.net/2007/02/family-day-and-family-meetings/.

Chapter 10 RELATIONSHIPS AT WORK

Blanchard, Ken, Carlos, John P., and Randolph, Alan, *Empowerment Takes More Than a Minute*, Berrett-Koehler Publishers, San Francisco, Calif., 1996.

Blanchard, Kenneth and Johnson, Spencer, *The One Minute Manager*, Berkley Books, New York, 1981.

Blanchard, Kenneth and Peale, Norman Vincent, *The Power of Ethical Management*, Fawcett Crest, New York, 1988.

Blanchard, Kenneth, Oncken Jr., William, and Burrows, Hal, *The One Minute Manager Meets the Monkey*, Quill William Morrow, New York, 1989.

Coyhis, Don, "*Medicine Wheel Teachings for Healthy Organizations, Servant Leadership*", Audiotapes, Moh-he-con-nuck, Inc., 1993.

Covey, Stephen R., *The 7 Habits of Highly Effective People -- Powerful Lessons in Personal Change*, Simon & Schuster, New York, 1989.

Covey, Stephen R., *Principle-Centered Leadership*, Simon & Schuster, New York, 1990

Feigelson, Sheila, *Energize Your Meetings with Laughter*, Association for Supervision and Curriculum Development, Alexandria, Virginia, 1998.

Goecke. Jo, "Bullies in the Workplace: A National Epidemic of Workers Pitted Against Workers Over Job Security", Women at Work, iSyndicate.com, Aug 18, 2000, available at http://www.workplacebullying.org/press/goecke1.html., (Retrieved May 2, 2011).

His Holiness the Dalai Lama, *How to See Yourself as You Really Are*, Atria, New York, 2006.

Namie, Gary and Namie, Ruth, "Stop the Jerks, Weasels & Snakes from Killing Your Organization", John Wiley & Sons, Inc., Hoboken, N.J., 2011.

Palmer, Parker J., *Let Your Life Speak, Listening for the Voice of Vocation*, John Wiley & Sons, Inc., Hoboken, N.J., 2000.

Patterson, Kerry, Grenny, Joseph, McMillan, Ron, and Switzler, Al, *Crucial Conversations: Tools for Talking When Stakes are High*, McGraw-Hill, Columbus, Ohio, 2002.

Roberts, Wess, *Victory Secrets of Attila the Hun*, Dell Publishing, New York, 1993.

Schaef, Anne Wilson and Fassel, Diane, *The Addictive Organization, Why We Overwork, Cover Up, Pick Up the Pieces, Please the Boss, & Perpetuate Sick Organizations*, Harper, San Francisco, 1988.

Scott, Cynthia D. and Jaffe, Dennis T., *Empowerment, A Practical Guide for Success*, Crisp Publications, Inc., Menlo Park, Calif., 1991.

"Stop Hate", available at http://www.stophate.org.

Tracy, Diane, *Blue's Clues for Success, The 8 Secrets Behind a Phenomenal Business*, Dearborn Trade Publishing, Chicago, Ill., 2002.

Weiss, Donald H., *How to Deal with Difficult People*, American Management Association, Amacon Books, New York, 1987.

Chapter 11 HOW TO STAY IN LOVE (PRACTICALLY) FOREVER

Fromm, Erich, *The Art of Loving*, Harper & Row, New York, 1956.

Grayson, Henry, *Mindful Loving -- 10 Practices for Creating Deeper Connections*, Penguin Group, New York, 2003.

Huston, Ted, "What's Love Got to do With It?", University of Texas, Austin feature story, available at http://www.utexas.edu/features/archive/2003/love.html, 2003.

Lerner, Harriet, *The Dance of Connection -- How to Talk to Someone When You're Mad, Hurt, Scared, Frustrated, Insulted, Betrayed, or Desperate*, Quill, 2001.

Parker-Pope, Tara, *For Better: The Science of a Good Marriage*, Penguin Group, New York, 2010.

Powell, John, *The Secret of Staying in Love -- Loving Relationships through Communication*, Thomas More, Allen, Texas, 1974.

Sarma, Kamal, *Mental Resilience, The Power of Clarity, How to Develop the Focus of a Warrior and the Peace of a Monk*, New World Library, Novato, Calif., 2008.

Schultz, Mort and the Editors of Consumer Reports Books, *Keep Your Car Running Practically Forever, An Easy Guide to Routine Care and Maintenance*, Consumers Reports Books, Yonkers, New York, 1991.

Seaward, Brian Luke, *Stressed is Desserts Spelled Backward -- Rising Above Life's Challenges with Humor, Hope, and Courage*, Conari Press, Berkeley, Calif., 1999.

Seaward, Brian Luke, *Quiet Mind, Fearless Heart, The Taoist Path through Stress and Spirituality*, John Wiley & Sons, Inc., Hoboken, N.J., 2004.

Thich Nhat Hanh, (translated by Sherab Chodzin Kohn), *True Love*, Shambhala, Boston, 2004.

The Living Bible, Paraphrased, I Corinthians 13:4 - 7 (TLB), Tyndale House Publishers, Illinois, 1971.

Section IV.
SPEED BUMPS

Chapter 12 HOW STRESS WORKS

Charles, C. Leslie and Donaldson, Mimi, *Bless Your Stress: It Means You're Still Alive!* Yes! Press, East Lansing, MI, 2006.

Du, Jing, McEwen, Bruce, and Manji, Husseini K., "Glucocorticoid receptors modulate mitochondrial function: A novel mechanism for neuroprotection", Communicative and Integrative Biology, 2(4): 350-352., (July - Aug 2009).

Grayson, Henry, *Mindful Loving -- 10 Practices for Creating Deeper Connections*, Penguin Group, New York, 2003.

McEwen, Bruce, with Lasley, Elizabeth Norton, *The End of Stress as We Know It*, Joseph Henry Press, Washington, D.C., 2002.

Seaward, Brian Luke, *Stressed is Desserts Spelled Backward, Rising Above Life's Challenges with Humor, Hope, and Courage*, Conari Press, Berkeley, CA, 1999.

Selye, Hans, *The Stress of Life*, McGraw-Hill Book Co., New York, 1956.

Chapter 13 A WORD ABOUT FEAR

Dyer, Wayne W., *Change Your Thoughts – Change Your Life*, Hay House, Inc., Carlsbad, Calif., 2007 (Tao Te Ching Translation).

McClelland, D.D., "Motivational Factors in Health and Disease", American Psychologist, (1989) 44 (4): 675-83.

Seaward, Brian Luke, *Quiet Mind, Fearless Heart, The Taoist Path through Stress and Spirituality*, John Wiley & Sons, Inc, Hoboken, New Jersey, 2004.

Chapter 14 EXPECTATIONS

The Holy Bible, King James Version

CHANGE

Dyer, Dr. Wayne W., *Change Your Thoughts – Change Your Life*, Hay House, Inc., Carlsbad, CA, 2007 (Tao Te Ching Translation).

"Erickson's Developmental Stages", available at AllPsych Online, http://allpsych.com/psychology101/social_development.html.

STRONG EMOTIONAL REACTIONS

Bhagavad-Gita Trust 1998 - 2009 U.S.A., available at http://www.bhagavad-gita.org/Gita/verse-04-18.html, Retrieved August 12, 2012.

Charles, C. Leslie and Donaldson, Mimi, *Bless Your Stress, It Means You're Still Alive!*, Yes! Press, East Lansing, Mich, 2006.

ILLNESS AND PAIN

"Coping with Grief and Loss: Understanding the Grieving Process". Retrieved from http://helpguide.org/mental/grief_loss.htm, (July 15, 2012).

Grayson, Henry, *Mindful Loving -- 10 Practices for Creating Deeper Connections*, Penguin Group, New York, 2003.

National Center for Complementary and Alternative Medicine website, available at http://nccam.nih.gov/.

Thich Nhat Hanh, (translated by Sherab Chodzin Kohn), *True Love*, Shambhala, Boston, 2004.

Section V
ARE WE THERE YET?

Chapter 15 TAKING ACTION

Chiaverini, Jennifer, *The New Year's Quilt*, Simon & Schuster, New York, 2007

"Coping with Grief and Loss: Understanding the Grieving Process.", Retrieved from http://helpguide.org/mental/grief_loss.htm, (July 15, 2012).

"How To Cope With Pain", website, available at http://www.howtocopewithpain.org/.

Mpabwanimana, Joel, Personal Communication, 2012.

Chapter 16 THE FRUITS OF LIVING WELL: STORIES AND WORDS OF WISDOM

Csikszentmihalyi, Mihaly, *FLOW: The Psychology of Optimal Experience*, Harper & Row, Publishers, New York, 1990.

Dyer, Wayne W., *Change Your Thoughts – Change Your Life*, Hay House, Inc., Carlsbad, Calif., 2007 (Tao Te Ching Translation).

Grayson, Henry, *Mindful Loving -- 10 Practices for Creating Deeper Connections*, Penguin Group, New York, 2003.

Hallowell, Edward M., *The Childhood Roots of Adult Happiness, Five Steps to Help Kids Create and Sustain Lifelong Joy*, Ballantine Books, New York, 2002.

Powell, John, *Fully Human, Fully Alive*, Argus Communications, Niles, Ill, 1976.

Sarma, Kamal, *Mental Resilience, The Power of Clarity -- How to Develop the Focus of a Warrior and the Peace of a Monk*, New World Library, Novato, Calif., 2008.

Seligman, Martin E.P., *Authentic Happiness*, cited in Pink, Daniel H., *A Whole New Mind – Why Right-Brainers Will Rule The World*, Riverhead Books, New York, 2005.

Schumaker, Bob, Available at An American Experience, available at http://www.pbs.org/wgbh/amex/honor/sfeature/sf_tap.html.

Thich Nhat Hanh, *Essential Writings*, Orbis Books, Maryknoll, New York, 2001.

This Emotional Life: In Search of Ourselves…and Happiness, Hosted by Daniel Gilbert, Vulcan Productions, Program on PBS, , 2010.

APPENDIX 1
Choosing a Therapist

Browning, Diane, "Guidelines for Choosing a Psychotherapist or Counselor", available at http://www.findacounselor.net/therapist-guidelines.html.

Good Therapy.org, available at http://www.goodtherapy.org/types-of-therapy.html.

Marriage counseling, available at www.Mayoclinic.com.

Singer, Jack N., "Helpful Guidelines for Choosing the Right Therapist", available at http://www.4therapy.com/life-topics/therapists-perspectives/helpful-guidelines-choosing-right-therapist-2782.

APPENDIX 2
Maslow's Hierarchy of Human Needs

Maslow, Abraham, "A Theory of Human Motivation", Psychological Review 1943, 50(4): 370-96.

APPENDIX 3
Abusive Relationships

Grayson, Henry, *Mindful Loving -- 10 Practices for Creating Deeper Connections*, Penguin Group, New York, 2003.

Help guide is available at http://helpguide.org/mental/domestic_violence_abuse_help_treatment_prevention.htm, (Retrieved Aug 19, 2009).

National Domestic Violence Hotline, 1-800-799-SAFE.

Recovery information is available at http://www.recovery-man.com/abusive/abusive.html, (Retrieved Aug 19, 2009).

U.S. Department of Agriculture, Domestic Violence Awareness Handbook, available at http://www.dm.usda.gov/shmd/aware.htm

Women's Law.org, available at www.womenslaw.org

Index

A

abundance 11, 21, 22, 31, 39, 88
affirmations 38, 39, 42, 43
anger 3, 25, 36, 76, 77, 79, 109
apology 49, 82
attitude 1, 38, 57, 82, 96, 119, 123, 125, 161, 173, 202, 206
attitude of gratitude 39, 41, 177, 205

B

balance 3, 18, 28, 31, 32, 47, 53, 54, 87, 95, 96, 98, 99, 100, 101, 105, 111, 112, 121, 137, 166, 193, 195, 202, 206, 208
barriers 32, 118, 182, 184, 185
boundaries 7, 64, 89, 95, 104, 159, 172
bullies 137, 138

C

change 7, 15, 28, 32-33, 40, 60-62, 75, 80-82, 96, 113, 119, 159, 173, 177, 179-180, 185-187, 189, 191-192, 202
changing habits 101-102, 201
communication 19, 44, 47, 48, 49, 84, 92, 137, 142, 145, 146, 180, 183
compassion 22, 31, 50, 70, 71, 72, 74, 76, 78, 80, 111, 119, 125, 127, 137, 144, 147, 148, 149, 174, 177, 189, 199
connected 18, 53, 56, 117, 118, 147, 167, 169, 189, 195, 207, 208
contentment 1, 2, 5, 11, 192, 208
coping 31, 44, 170, 193, 202
courage 31, 146, 168, 183, 189

D

depression 2, 5, 15, 73, 79, 100, 111, 118, 159, 170, 194, 195
discipline 24, 44, 91, 127, 128, 129, 130, 131
distress 70, 79, 83, 144, 161

E

Eagle Meditation Exercise 60, 61, 62
ego 2, 6, 24, 25, 36, 37, 49, 53, 56, 82, 88, 117, 126, 143, 187, 190, 192
emotional health 49, 92, 111, 129, 147, 175, 193
empowerment 208
Enoughness Principle, The 38, 88
Exercise 97-101
expectations 67, 135, 143, 159, 179
Eye Movement Desensitization Reprograming 15

F

fear 1, 2, 3, 25, 36, 37, 45, 65, 70, 71, 72, 82, 83, 104, 137, 159, 161, 165, 166, 168, 174, 182, 183, 186, 189, 190, 202, 203, 208, 213
fight-or-flight response 44, 160, 161
forgiveness 18, 31, 70, 75, 76, 77, 78, 81, 83, 85, 206

G

grief, grieving 1, 2, 3, 112, 166, 190, 194, 195

H
hope 2, 7, 13, 17, 31, 81, 166, 168, 195, 208, 210, 211

humor 31, 214

I
illness 78, 159, 160, 171, 173, 192, 193

inner resources 31

J
journaling 6, 32, 44, 161

K
kindness 31, 70, 71, 73, 74, 76, 127, 147, 202, 208

L
listening 4, 47, 58, 72, 147

love 6, 7, 11, 17, 18, 21, 22, 26, 28, 31, 36, 37, 38, 39, 45, 53, 69, 70, 72, 73, 82, 87, 88, 91, 105, 118, 119, 121, 122, 123, 125, 126, 127, 130, 131, 141, 142, 143, 144, 145, 146, 147, 148, 157, 165, 174, 179, 189, 190, 199, 202, 203, 205, 207, 208, 223, 232

M
magical thinking 5

maturational changes 159, 186, 191

meditation 7, 40, 53, 55, 56, 57, 58, 63, 91, 99, 106, 167

mindfulness 31, 53, 63, 64, 65, 208

mind rut 38, 56, 59, 79

money 12, 90, 96, 97, 121, 166, 173, 191, 206, 208, 225, 231, 233

Mother Teresa Effect, The 174

N
nutrition 19, 101, 102, 113, 121, 173, 175

O
Oneness 56

P
passion 39, 53, 157, 201, 213, 214, 215

patience 31, 73, 87

positive thinking 35, 37, 161

postmaterialistic values 22

powwow 51, 52, 146

purpose in life 18-20, 23, 53, 55, 56, 125, 162, 192, 199

S
self-actualization 11

self-esteem 138

Serenity Prayer, The 180

simplicity 18, 31, 54, 88, 91, 208

sleep 53, 87, 91, 92, 95, 99, 100, 121, 167, 169, 173, 195, 230

spiritual muscles 18, 31, 146

spirituality
    attention to 22, 55
    stress and 89

stress
    acute vs. chronic 70, 160
    coping with change 186
    disease and 44, 76, 87, 159, 161
    ego and 25
    spirituality and 89, 91

Sure Enough Principle, The 36

T
Tai Chi 57, 58, 98, 99, 100, 101, 135, 193

tears 59, 112, 167

technostress 89

time management 87, 95, 96, 113, 121

U

unconditional love 45, 127, 142, 144, 148

V

values 22, 32, 48, 79, 162, 183

victim vs. victor 2, 25, 27, 28, 35, 37, 38, 77, 78, 88, 131, 138, 157, 173, 190, 225, 227

volunteering 111

W

work life 32, 96, 104, 105, 119, 135, 136, 137, 138

About the Author

Elaine Scribner is living her passions: writing, teaching weaving and loving. She is devoted to living life to the fullest and cultivating tools that create a joyous life. Twenty-plus years ago, in the space of five years, she faced cancer, divorce, homelessness, loss of her mother to lung cancer and being laid off twice in quick succession. She discovered that joy really is a state of mind and is there for the embracing.

Elaine is the founder and CEO of Cartwheels, Inc., providing worksite wellness programs, wellness coaching and workshops. She has created *CartWheels*, a game implementing play, laughter and creativity, and for her latest endeavor, she has authored the book *Stride Like a Lion, Soar Like an Eagle: A Companion Guide to Living Joyously*.

Other hats she enthusiastically juggles are those of professional speaker, college professor, holistic stress management instructor, hospice nurse, lay minister, weaver, gardener and, most importantly, mom.

The last page is dedicated to Rosalyn who said when I was getting ready to send out more chapters…."Great, because I want to know how the book ends…."

So….be the lion
….be the eagle

And may you soar, not just fly
And may you roar, not just try

As we stride joyously, lovingly and contentedly into the sunset … mindful and fully present

(˘ ˑ.(˘ ˑ ͒.ˊˊ)ˎˊˊ)
«˚˚*… ☺ …*˚˚»
(ˎˊˊ(ˎˊˊˊ˘ ˑ.)˘ ˑ.)